I0683066

GANGA REVIEW

2022

Ganga Review ISSN 1930-0662 is published annually in the United States by Chintamani Books. The journal is a member of the Community of Literary Magazines and Presses. Issues are printed in accordance with the Sustainable Forestry Initiative. For every magazine purchased, a tree is planted.

Submission Guidelines: Please submit up to five poems or one work of prose per envelope. Include SASE and contact information (name, address, telephone, email). Work should be previously unpublished. We accept first North American serial rights. Kindly post to Submittable.

Address correspondence to:

Lalitamba
P.O. Box 131
Planetarium Station
New York, NY 10024

Subscriptions are $12 for one year, plus $4.50 postage and handling.

Lalitamba is a 501(c)3 nonprofit organization. The journal is donated to prisons and communities in need throughout the United States. Proceeds from magazine sales are used for these charitable purposes, including shelter for vulnerable women and prison book distribution. Further contributions are tax-deductible according to New York State law.

Website: www.lalitamba.com
Facebook: https://www.facebook.com/Lalitamba-252686692751/

The opinions expressed by contributors do not reflect those of the Editor.

Ganga Review
© 2022 Chintamani Books
P.O. Box 131, Planetarium Station
New York, NY 10024
All rights reserved.

ISBN 978-1-7324541-2-5

The journal was inspired by a bhajan sung on a pilgrimage through India. In early 2004, we traveled through the country with India's "hugging saint" to alleviate the suffering that comes with poverty, illness, and plain loss of hope. The journal was founded when we returned to New York City in November of that year.

The journal is named for the sacred Ganga River, an expression of Divine Mother.

TABLE OF CONTENTS

Essays

Art

LETTERS AND PRAYERS

Sanguine squire, aesthetically mired,
Hidden away he stays.
Odd man out, until admired,
To Him we sing our praise.

Entrenched in black, suspended in back,
He pines to intervene.
And when he does, they're back on track,
Uprooted from ravine.

Gregarious sheep, the shepherd doth keep,
But He unto his own.
A punctured soul, where air can weep,
He clouts the hole alone.

His purpose is driven,
As we are forgiven.

Charles March III
San Juan Capistrano, CA

Dear Lord, we pray for a drought
to descend onto this water city
of hulls and paddles
and crumbling palaces.

A city that wears time like a mask
and space like breath.
Who could conceive such a place?
Not I, born in a far-distant motor town.

Here, there are no cars or buses,
no trucks or motorcycles,
no battery-powered skateboards.
There are no streets.

Dear Lord, we pray for a drought,
a *siccità* of fiery air and parched soil,
but heavy weather shrouds the night.

White stone, white beauty,
a barefoot bridge spans a quiet canal,
like myth wed to nature
above heavenly wisdom.

Dear Lord, we pray for safety
but our hearts long for wilderness.

We pray for a tide of mercy,
for the skill and vision
to save this city.

We pray for a drought.
We pray for the beautiful necessity.

Patrick Pfister
Barcelona, Spain

The journal is an offering for liberation.
May all beings be joyful and free.

Emily Adair

HOW TO TAME A BEAST

OCTOBER 20, 2001

THERE IS A BEAST INSIDE everyone. Every man, woman, and child. It is something animal. Something caged. Something visceral. It is something to be wary of, but do not be afraid of it. Maybe you've already met yours, and maybe you know it by name. Maybe you think I am lying, but I challenge you to look deep inside. In the back caverns of your body, just below your heart and to left, you will feel a cage. And that is where the beast lives. Now, he doesn't have to live there, and there is a way to set him free, but because he is in fact a part of you, it may hurt a little. Or it may hurt a lot. You must fight him, if you want live. Only you can silence him. Only you can set him free. But you need not do it alone.

MARCH 11, 2000

THE WEEDS AROUND THE HOUSE, wet with rain, bow to the coming summer. The whole world is a watercolor, and I am washed out by the long year. Mom turns her laptop towards me. Before looking, I know onscreen is a community college. This one is in Bellingham, called Whatcom Community College. Yesterday, she showed me Skagit Valley Community College, and the day before, it was Everett Community College.

"That looks like a fun one. You should go," I say, my voice as monotone as possible, glancing up from my sheet music.

She sighs. "Seth, You need to think about this. Summer will be here and gone before you know it."

"Send me the link," I say, mainly to shut her up. I will never look at it.

She is exasperated with my lack of drive. Every day since I turned 15 she has reminded me how far a college education can take you. She receives pamphlets from all the nearby schools, as well as bordering states. She reads through them like a kid with the J.C. Penney catalogue, as if she were picking out what she wants for Christmas, circling programs that would be good for me or clubs she finds intriguing. She did it for Eddie and Parker, as well. The idea of Eddie going to college makes me laugh. He is the rebel middle child. To Parker, however, Mom is God. She went to the school Mom wanted her to attend and follows her ideas like they are the law of the Bible. She is the perfect one. Eddie resents her for it, but I don't really care.

Mom focuses on me now, because I am all she has. And I resent it. If Dad were still here, things would be different. Better. As she gets up to go make a cup of tea, I can tell she is irritated. I take my saxophone and sheet music into my room to avoid an argument.

MARCH 26, 2000

THE CONVERSATIONS WITH MOM have become more and more intense. It's like her life depends on what I do with mine. People at church are asking those dreaded questions, still. The most common question is, "Seth, what are you doing after graduation?" I hate this one the most. Second most popular is, "Seth, how's Ed doing? I hear he had another run in with the law." Third is, "How is Parker doing with her studies?" The more time passes, the more I am sure there is no life for me here. I will never be who these people want me to be, who Mom wants me to be.

MARCH 29, 2000

IT HAS BEEN FOUR YEARS to the day. The old deck creaks, as I step onto the wet wood. An old lawn mower is slumped to the left. To the right is Eddie's boxing area. Tied to the wall of the pallet shed is a thin white towel. It is blood-spackled and crusty.

With that thought, I pull back and punch the dirty, blood-spackled towel as hard as I can. There is less padding than I hoped. I let the pain emanate through my knuckles. I punch again. There is a rush. My body feels alive, like there is a fire coursing through my veins, down through my toes and fingertips. It feels good. Destructive, but good.

With every punch, my knuckles get bloody and bruised. I can barely open or close my hands. It feels like they will be stuck in fists forever. I spend a full hour that day in Eddie's boxing area, but I do not leave the same. I have awakened something that I don't know if I can silence.

SEPTEMBER 25, 2000

I HAVE ONLY BEEN ON THE ROAD for two weeks, but it feels like a lifetime. I left on a Tuesday. I just packed my truck and left. I told her I was going to the store for cigarettes, and I never came back. Now, I am driving the winding road, south along the 101. The radio reception goes in and out. I turn the knob to off and listen to the rain that bounces across the rusty roof of my truck. I look at the bright green clock on the car stereo. It reads 10:42p.m. To the left,

I see a lot that looks like a promising place to park for the night. I pull over. Being alone is comforting right now. Of the thoughts that swarm my head, the most prominent is of my mom sitting at home all alone. "Aw, screw her," I say out loud, hitting the steering wheel. Sometimes, I feel guilty that I left. Sometimes, I hate her. As I feel my emotions rise, I turn the radio knob back on to listen to the static. The voices in my head never tell me what I want to hear. When I think about home, there is a pressure, a vicious pulling deep down in my chest. I try to ignore it, but tonight guilt gnaws at me like a beast on a bone. It's best not to think about home.

NOVEMBER 17, 2000

DESPITE THE VICIOUS COLD that always finds a way to claw through my clothing and skin, the market in Portland is surprisingly active. I hold my saxophone and play. My fingers are almost numb, but I can still feel the prickles. Some people stay and listen to me. Others don't care. Playing the sax is my one source of joy and income. Mom always told me it was a waste of time. "Musician's don't make good money, Son," she would say. "'Let's try to think of a more realistic career." God, I hate her. I wish she could see me now. Would she be proud? I push her from my mind, focusing on my fingers and breath.

Dad would be proud. He loved music more than anything. Even in his wheelchair, he could still play, but after the accident at the wood shop, he changed. I remember sitting in the hospital room with him. There is a cold much like the Portland cold now that surrounds that memory. His hand had been crushed to the point that he would never be able to play the piano again. It hung limply from his arm. I saw him weep that day for the first time.

Everything went downhill after that. I remember watching the depression eat at him every day after that, picking at his flesh and muscle until it was chewing on his bones. It finally ate him whole, hand and all.

I focus on my breath and listen to the sound of my saxophone, as it emanates out and up and over. I wish I could go with that sound, to float on the air and cease to exist. Maybe that's how he felt when he pulled the trigger. Ave Maria was set on repeat when we found him. This is the song I play now. Inside, my chest feels like it is being ripped apart, but I keep playing. It is all I can do.

FEBRUARY 19, 2001

I HAVE BEEN LIVING JUST OUTSIDE of San Francisco since early January. My hair hangs in matted curls, wisping around my face. Even in the sun of California, the Portland cold is with me. It crawled so deep into my body that now it can't get out. It sits in my gut and rattles an invisible cage. The sand feels soft beneath my bare feet, as I play a jazzy tune. I close my eyes and grab the sand with my toes. The feeling of the sand distracts me from the urge to stop playing and cry. It is getting harder and harder to continue playing. Even the joy the music brings is starting to die off, like flies in the winter with nowhere warm to live. I push my curls behind my ear when then song ends and sit down in the sand.

"How long have you been playing?" I hear someone behind me ask. I turn. He is an older gentleman. His hair is greying, a rough dark grey similar to the color of a dog's coat. He is wearing a dark green t-shirt and tan cargo shorts.

I stutter over my words. "Uh, about since I was eight," I say squinting in the sunlight.

He sits down next to me. This surprises me. Most people throw money into my saxophone case, but they rarely talk to me.

"My son played," he says, looking at me. "He was damn good, too. Hearing you reminds me of him. Thank you."

I contemplate responding with something beyond *you're welcome* or *thank you*. In a moment, I realize how very long it has been since I've had a conversation of any depth or meaning with anyone. The thought entices me. After a long silence, I ask, "Why doesn't he play anymore?"

"Died. Suicide. He was 23. His mother and I didn't expect it at all. We thought he was pretty happy kid."

I don't know how to respond. I feel my face go red. My body quietly shakes, and I stare at the sand. It is all I can do to hold back the tears. "I am sorry for your loss." I say. Then I get up and walk back to my truck. Once in the bed, safe from the world, I sob.

JULY 6, 2001

THE HEAT OF THE DAY is sinking into the ocean. I have the canopy window open to let the breeze dance through the stagnant air in my truck. I am lying on my bed and drifting in and out of sleep. I've been buying weed from a guy named Lonnie. He gives me a good price, better than most. I finally understand why Eddie smoked so much in high school. When I smoke, the clawing in my chest goes numb. I know it will be there when the high wears off, but the temporary relief is better than the constant pain. Scrunching up into a ball, I close my eyes. Pictures flood my subconscious. I see the pastures where I grew up. I am covered in blood, and my bones are protruding. I am at my old church, but no one sees me. No one comments on my broken and bloodied body. They all have buckets of white paint. Stroke after stroke, they paint over my blood and my bones. And they are satisfied. All I know is that I miss my dad, and I want my mom to be proud of me. And then I am child, sobbing in someone's arms. As I slip into sleep, and the pictures cease, I feel my chest for a heart beat. I can't find one. And that gives me peace. Maybe I'll die in my sleep.

OCTOBER 14, 2001

HE HANDS ME $2000 in cash. It is mostly hundreds, but a few twenties as well. I hand over the keys and watch him climb into my truck and drive away. My only belongings now are my saxophone and the clothes on my back. I open up my saxophone case to tuck the bills in. I know it would have made more sense to sell the sax and keep the truck, but I can't get rid of my instrument. This sax is my only joy, my only weapon against the darkness. I am holding onto it for dear life.

I am in Coeur d'Alene now. It is my favorite city. Every season is beautiful. I sit on the boardwalk and dangle my feet over the edge, leaning my head between the railing bars. Today is a special day, and I am alone for it. I quietly sing happy birthday to myself.

Maybe, with the cash, I'll go buy myself a cake.

I feel a hand on my shoulder. I am sure it is a cop asking me to leave. People like me dirty up the area. I turn around and open my mouth to tell him I'll move. When I see the face looking down at me, I just stare. It is Eddie. We are frozen in that moment. His eyes are full of surprise. Without words, he sits down on the ground with me.

He looks different than he did when I left two years ago. Younger. Finally, he says, "Happy birthday."

I chuckle. "Thanks."

"I was thinking of you. I wondered if you would be here. Man, where ya been?"

"Around," I say, looking back at the lake. I feel awkward, dirty. Like he should be mad at me for leaving. I feel like I don't quite know how to speak. The words on my tongue feel heavy and poisonous.

"And where have you been?" I retort, releasing the poison from my lips. I don't know why, but I am angry.

"Mostly living back home. I got a job as a landscaper. Good enough money. I like working with my hands, and it keeps me out of trouble."

I open and close my hands. I am pulsing with anger at anything and everything. My body feels taken over. I think of the rush back in the pallet shed with the dirty, blood-spackled towel. Before I know what I am doing, my hand is in a fist. I swing around and punch Eddie straight in the mouth. As my fist slides off his face, it throbs. He turns away, opening and closing his jaw. He is silent, looking away and to the left. I just sit there, breathing hard, trying to figure out why I punched my brother, why there is an undying rage inside me. What is wrong with me? Should I run away?

Eddie is the first to speak. He takes a deep breath. "I know how you feel. I was there too, you know. When Dad died, it wasn't just you who was affected." His voice cracked a bit, and I watched his emotions begin to swim. " It hurt all of us, but you can't blame Mom, you can't blame Parker, and you can't blame me." He took a deep breath and exhaled. "Dad took his own life and left us to pick up his pieces. He was a coward. He was selfish." He almost spat those last words.

I shrug, "Yeah, or maybe he was just hopeless," I say. "Maybe he just needed some help." We are quiet again, looking out over the lake.

"Come home with me," he says, almost begs. I don't answer.

"Seth," he says again, "come home with me." This time it is more a command than a question.

I snort. "No, I disappointed her because I didn't go to college. I'm sure she hates me now. She needs everything to be perfect and nice. I am none of those things. I don't belong."

"Seth, it's okay not to be okay. It's not okay not to be there. Dad took the coward's way out. Don't follow his steps."

I begin to think about his words. He puts his hand on my shoulder. "Please?" As he looks deep into my eyes, I know I have to go. There is a strength inside that feels deeper than the anger, the depression, and the hollow fire. I know I have to go.

OCTOBER 15, 2001

AS WE PULL INTO THE DRIVEWAY, the knot that has been forming in my stomach since I got into Eddie's car begins to tighten, like a boa constrictor around its prey. My mother is so surprised to see me that she bursts into tears, touching and holding my face despite the grime and dirt I am covered in. As we walk into the house, I look around. A lot has changed.

The flowers in the front yard have always been pristine, even right after Dad's death. Now, there are weeds growing through all of the beds. When we enter the house, I see dust on the window sills and shelves. A pile of paintings are stacked on the dining room table, where I have never seen anything but seasonal placemats and centerpieces. The house feels lighter, like people live here now.

She brings me into the kitchen. "I made this yesterday, for you. In case you decided to come home." She opens the fridge. Inside, there is a birthday cake with my name on it and a little figure playing a saxophone.

"Thanks, Mom," I say.

I tell them a few stories—funny stories, sad stories from my journey. I feel alive, better than I have in years. This is better than weed. But there is still a clawing inside. The invisible cage is rattling, begging me to pay attention to it.

Late in the evening, when the conversation has lulled and we sit quietly watching "I love Lucy" reruns, I say that I am going out for a cigarette. The screen door slams, as I walk out.

Once inside the shed, the hurt, rage, and fear that have been my fuel begin banging against my insides, as if begging me to let them stay. I was small a year ago, but I feel smaller now. I have made so much room for the anger and depression that there is little room left for me. I look around. The dirty, blood-spackled towel is still there. Weeds are growing through the floor and walls. The wood is rotting. I step inside, and the floorboards sink.

In a strange way, I feel like I have entered my own soul.

As I approach the boxing area, my knees feel weak. My hands begin to shake. Before I can control myself, I fall and sob uncontrollably. My gut starts to turn in on itself, and I vomit onto the old, rotten wood. I grab my stomach tightly and sob.

I hear a rustle of footsteps outside. Turning, I see my mother standing in the doorway.

I gulp back my tears. "What do you want?" I bark, my throat sore.

She remains quiet, but steps forward. We stay like that for what feels like an uncomfortable amount of time. Then, she walks toward me with purpose and confidence. She kneels down beside me, wiping away the vomit and tears with her sleeve. "Son, this isn't who you are."

I look at the ground, unable to make eye contact with her.

She puts her arm around me. "But you have to understand something. I learned this after you left. After your father's death, I was scared. Scared to let everyone see how broken I truly was. I told myself I had to be strong, so you three could have a good life. But that fear turned into a lie I was living every day. I started pushing that lie onto you. Let me tell you something. There is a beast inside everyone. Every man, woman, and child. It is something animal. Something caged. Something visceral. Something instinctual. It is something to be wary of, but not anything to fear. Listen, though. The beast doesn't have to live there, and there is a way to set him free. Because he is still a part of you, it may hurt a little. Or it may hurt a lot. After you left, I had to face my beast. He almost destroyed me. Don't let him destroy you."

She took a deep breath. "I am sorry, for all the times I didn't allow you to be broken, because I was afraid of how others would look at me. I am sorry I didn't create a safe space for you."

I hang on her every word. It is all I have needed to hear since Dad's suicide six years ago. I begin to cry again, this time quiet tears of surrender. As I surrender, I can feel the beast of depression, anger, and sorrow slip through my fingers and toes. I feel my body loosen and relax. I feel alive again. I breathe deeply, and I finally look at my mother. "I love you," I say through sobs.

"I love you too," she responds, leaning her head against mine.

OCTOBER 19, 2001

I AM SITTING ATOP my favorite tree with my saxophone in hand. I play as one who has come out of the darkness. I play as one rescued. I let the wind wisp my hair about like it did in California, but this wind brings peace.

As I play, I think of my Dad. I stop and pull the reed out of my mouth. Out loud I say, " I forgive you for leaving. I'm sure they have pianos in heaven. I love you." And I know he hears me. I know he is proud.

Faiz Ahmad

A BRIEF HISTORY OF BURIALS

The ancients had
elaborate burials;
near the skulls,
they placed shell rings

and pots, jasper
stones, jewelry
and what not—
preparations for afterlife.

In our times
to do such things
would be preposterous,
laughable.

We keep our
burials simple
and vague

yet when we reach
a particular age,
with blood as
shovel

we sweat through
the apocalyptic night
excavating hard
our own souls

as if looking for
certain precious
buried objects
to save us

on a later day.

Ghaliya Hasan
Essam M. Al-Jassim, Translator

THE LOVING EYE

"What do you like most about me?"
  she asked him for the thousandth time.

"Why do you ask me that question every day?" he replied.

"Because every time I ask you,
  you come up with a new answer!"

Ahmed Shaker

Essam M. Al-Jasim, Translator

THE LAST MOMENTS OF A BRAVE MOUSE

JUST BEFORE THE SUN went down during dinner, Hassan shrieked and pointed. "It's the mouse! The mouse!"

"Where is it?" Ali asked.

"I saw it, too," Sami said. "It ran under the sofa."

"The sofa? Great." Ahmed sighed.

Hassan grinned. "It's the mouse's unlucky day. Its life must come to an end. This time, it won't escape us."

They quickly got up, put aside their food, closed the door, and tightly sealed the gap under the door with a piece of worn old cloth. It was a total blockade. They were all on the alert, heedful and ready.

Ahmed grabbed a shoe, Hassan grabbed a stick, and Sami grabbed a broom; whereas Ali just raised his hand in a standby position.

The mouse clung to the upper part of the sofa leg and remained there.

"Who starts?" Ahmed asked.

"Hassan, go ahead," Sami said.

"No, let Ali start."

"Me?"

Hassan nodded. "Yes. Just shake the sofa, and we'll snatch it."

Ali tiptoed forward and then jolted the sofa. A whisper of movement was quickly followed by a faint squeak and scratching. After another movement, there was silence. Shoe, stick, broom, and clenched hand were all ready for action.

"It's there, clutching the top corner," Hassan said.

"What a mischievous mouse!" Ahmed exclaimed.

THE MOUSE LOOKED OUT at them and considered the course of events. They're dreaming, he thought.

"You'll never reach me. It's not the first time I've gotten away, you bastards. What have I really done, though? I've just eaten pitiful pieces of stale bread crumbs, the refrigerator power cord, Ali's shirt, Hassan's pants, and Ahmed's copy of Animal Physiology, which he didn't return to the university library—simple things. What a poverty-stricken place and a bunch of stupid people."

Even though the mouse didn't dwell on these matters, Ali caught him by surprise by banging the top of the sofa with his hand.

What a sordid person, the mouse thought as he scurried under the sofa to the far corner.

"It reached the corner," Hassan said. "Sami, use the broomstick and move it from side to side. Then, we'll overtake it."

"Good idea," said Ali.

"I told you. You won't catch me." The mouse stuck out his tongue at them.

"Move away," Ahmed cautioned his friends.

"Let's turn the sofa upside down," Sami suggested.

"Turn it over?" Hassan asked. "Bright idea. But who's going to do it? Me? No way. Ali, you can do it. No? Okay, Ahmed. Neither you nor Sami can do it? Okay let's all do it together. One, two, three . . . go!"

They all turned their attention to the space under the sofa.

How unexpected, the flustered mouse thought. Damned human mind—root of all evil, death, and destruction. What should I do? Should I go out?

"Aren't you ashamed of yourselves? Four against one. Have you lost your senses completely? I'm a palm-sized creature."

Is manliness dying? Should I confront them? Yes, I should. I should come out and hide somewhere. But where? Their lounge is dilapidated—an old chest of drawers, two chairs, and a sofa. Think, think . . . go out.

The mouse leapt and ran up the leg of Ali's pants. No one saw him, but Ali felt him scamper to the top of his pants, heading for his sensitive area.

"Oh, my leg. Son of a bitch. Catch it. My leg."

Sami frowned. "Your leg? Where?"

"It's in my pants. Damn, it's running. Catch it—Ah!" Ali screamed while everyone was unable to control their laughter. He then captured the mouse with his right hand, but it bit him.

Ali looked at his thumb and screamed, "It's blood."

He threw the mouse to the ground. Badly hurt and bloodied, the animal slipped into unconsciousness.

The mouse saw the Ghost of Death approach him, as the humans struck him with the shoe, stick, broom, and a series of quick kicks.

With his last dying breath, the mouse muttered, "Lousy human bastards. It doesn't really matter, anyway. I've lived my whole life as I should have, and now I'm dying as my father died with honor."

Paul Bamberger

MIRROR

madman mirror's lengthening shadow
a tapping at the window
madman the lost child of the five and tens
    a story left untold
madman wits sharpened on the everyday blows
they drive your dream away
madman weather the storms
the dream is meant to be
madman years in the abyss
liberty liberty liberty
madman crying out is of no use
       hysteria is what brings them here
madman prepare yourself
      they are not who they seem to be

Steve Carr

STILL LIFE

JORGE SITS ON AN UPENDED WOODEN CRATE near the entrance of Fisherman's Wharf. His fingers are covered with different colors of chalk that over the years has turned his fingertips gray. A streak of green is smudged across his right cheek. As the sun beats down on him, sweat drips from his hair onto the back of his neck and runs under his t-shirt and down his spine.

The white sheet of paper attached to the easel in front of him is glaring, so he tries to keep his eyes focused on the dark blue chalk he is using to color the woman's blouse. She sits on a crate and fidgets, constantly looking at her watch, while he draws her.

Finally, he sprays the drawing with fixative and announces, "All done."

The woman stands and receives a ten dollar bill from her husband, who has been waiting nearby, watching sea lions frolic on the rocks a short distance from the shoreline.

Jorge unclips the drawing from the easel and hands it to the woman. She and her husband stare at it for several moments. They do not speak, until at last the husband says to his wife, "It looks like you, sort of."

"It's not supposed to look exactly like me," she says. "It's a caricature."

She hands the money to Jorge, thanks him, and walks away with her husband.

Jorge tucks the money into a small burlap pouch with the thirty dollars he has already made that day and stuffs the pouch into his back pocket. He hides his crate behind a Fisherman's Wharf sign, the same place he always hides it. He folds the easel, places it with the drawing tablet under his arm, picks up the plastic toolbox filled with chalks and a can of fixative, and walks off toward Market Street.

THE BUS BENCH IS MADE of metal. Its green-tinted plastic roof offers shelter from the sun. Jorge clutches the bus fare in his hand. When the bus pulls up to the curb, the doors whoosh open. Several passengers emerge, their heads low, their eyes averted. Jorge climbs the stairs into the bus and slides a one dollar bill into the fare box. He watches as the chalk imprints of his fingertips on George Washington's face disappear into the machine. As soon as he sits down in the seat behind the driver, the doors close. The bus lurches forward and pulls out into traffic.

Glancing into the rearview mirror, the bus driver says, "You get rich, today, Jorge?"

"Not today, Simon," Jorge answers with a chuckle, "but I've earned enough to sleep another night on a bed in my own room."

Simon is a big man, and his body expands beyond the back of his seat like dough that has risen from a baking pan. His eyes dart in all directions. "You should get a real job," he says.

"I applied to be a nuclear scientist, but they said the position was filled," Jorge replies.

The woman in the seat across the aisle stares at Jorge. Her eye shadow is the same shade of green as the chalk on his cheek. She holds a black patent leather purse in her lap and nervously plays with the gold latch that keeps it closed. Although the inside of the bus is air conditioned, her skin glistens with sweat.

Jorge smiles and nods at her, but she only stares.

Eight blocks up Market Street, Simon pulls the bus to the curb and opens the door. "Stay out of trouble," he says to Jorge, who rises from his seat and descends the steps.

Jorge crosses Market Street, winding his way through the throng of workers heading home at the end of their work day. The breeze blowing in from the bay funnels between the large stores, hotels, and skyscrapers. The air is filled with the scent of sea water. He walks down a side street that takes him into the South of Market district. Here, the buildings are grayer, as if they are aging in a human way. There's no sign above the door to the hotel he enters. It opens to a flight of dimly lit stairs. The aroma of chlorinated floor cleaner hangs in the air. Pieces of chalk rattle against the sides of his toolbox with every step he takes. At the top of the stairs, he stops in front of the check-in desk, shielded by a wire screen. He peers through a small slot used for passing paperwork back and forth.

Lucinda is sitting on a stool and stares fixedly through the screen at the chalk on Jorge's face. "Honey, that color doesn't suit you," she says with a smoker's raspy voice. Her hair is dyed the color of butter and looks as if she had stuck her finger into a light socket. She hides her Adam's apple with a silk scarf. Several bracelets jingle on her thick wrists, as she waves her large hands.

Jorge brushes at his cheek, smearing the chalk smudge. "With what I earned today, I now have enough to pay this week's rent and send a few dollars home," he says.

"That's good, because otherwise I'd have to throw you and that squawking buzzard out onto the street," she says. "Texas almost broke your door down this afternoon trying to get into your room to strangle it."

"It's a parakeet," Jorge says. "Mr. Khan said it was okay that I keep Louise."

"Sweetheart, if I complain loud enough to Mr. Khan, you might as well make a nice hat out of Louise's feathers, because that bird and her never-ending chatter will be gone. Mr. Khan may own this hotel, but I run it. Understand?"

"Yes," Jorge says meekly. "I'll go get the rest of the money for the rent and be right back."

"I ain't going anywhere," she says nonchalantly.

Lucinda passes the room key through the slot, picks up an emery board, and begins to file her long, orange-lacquered fingernails.

Jorge walks down the long hallway lined with closed doors. From behind the doors come the muffled sounds of music on radios, laugh tracks from television sitcoms, and conversations spoken in different languages.

Texas comes out of the bathroom at the end of the hall. He's tall and lanky, and he strides toward Jorge in the same way a lion attacks a wounded zebra.

He jabs Jorge's chest with his finger. "I'm gonna kill that bird of yours," he says.

Jorge doesn't look into Texas' eyes. He has done that before and is certain he saw El Diablo. "Louise is just doing what a bird does," Jorge says. "I will try to teach her to be quieter."

"You do that. I'm not warning you again," Texas says. He turns and goes into his room, slamming the door.

Jorge unlocks the door to his room and walks in to the excited calls of Louise whose cage is covered with a bright yellow cloth. He closes the door and sets the easel, drawing tablet, and tool box down on the floor. He removes the cloth from the cage.

"*Hola mi amor*," he says to the bird.

Louise sticks her beak between the cage bars. She chirps softly, as he rubs her beak with his fingertips. He fills her food dish with birdseed and pours water from a plastic bottle into her water dish. Then, he turns and raises a window, allowing the noise from traffic and exhaust fumes from the street to rush into the room.

He takes the pouch of money from his pocket and sits down on the bed. Before he reaches down for his cash box, which holds the rest of the rent, he glances around at the drawings pinned to the walls. They are brightly colored, exquisitely rendered—chalk drawings of a cracked bowl, a white porcelain vase with a single dandelion, a gym shoe with a hole in the toe, and an empty Styrofoam food container. On another wall hang drawings of objects from home. A clay pot. A sombrero. His childhood toy drum.

Tomorrow, he will return to the wharf, find his hidden crate and sit again upon it, waiting for passersby to sit for him. He will make enough money, he hopes, for another few nights in this room.

He stares hard at the toy drum he so loved as a child. This is his life, somehow.

He catches sight of his face in the small mirror above his bed, and for a moment, he mistakes his reflection for a one of his caricatures.

Richard Alan Bunch

SCENT FROM AN ECSTATIC

At the Shearwater Bar and Grille,
we note a fruit basket and sweet
corn that hangs over a ceramic bowl's lip.

We order jacket potato, chicken salad,
and Calistoga water.

We hear the swish of sails,
espy gulls and other
far-wandering seabirds
that cry in the maritime sun
through the leaves of a cottonwood.

That the beauty
of the floating lotus
rises out of the mud
like precious pearl
is something we sense
even here in this Maine harbor.

Scanning the open sky,
we connect the dots
from the gleam
of unfamiliar years,
before numbers became
history's parchment of
radical characters to exo-planets
yet unseen but inferred.

We know outer space
is the homestead of suns
beyond our body's totem of joy,
where we may discover
something more intelligent than intellect,
something more spiritual than spirit.

This is what happens
when once you breathe in
the scent from an ecstatic.

Richard Alan Bunch

SCORPION SUN

As the horizon ripens
into memory pools
and fields wet
with diamond dew,
the day
is a scorpion sun
in a mindscape of bone.

The earth breaks hearts
with its nevers
and corduroy elbows,
yet blazes
with blond sellers
of plum brandy and
shadows of the sea.

This summer sows mumbles
of giraffes,
chirring swallows,
and cranes
in orchards
of spacious skies.

As the birch tree
rubs the wind,
you say *adios*
to an x-lady
and lift
to a higher love
after many
ten-round bouts
in hell.

You are not
a madman
but one
with three eyes open.

Holly Day
VISION

Jeffrey S. Chapman

THE GOOD FIGHT

IN THE MIDDLE OF THE 20TH CENTURY, as the country was emerging out of the Great Depression like a chick emerging from an egg, Centerville was moving in the other direction, more like an egg that had been cracked and scrambled. Before the Depression, the city had been glorious, an industrial hub situated along the first transcontinental railroad, rich with iron and coal. Workers arrived in waves. Skyscrapers rose like crops of wheat. But those days were long gone. People talked of its heyday as if it were a myth, a different time, with a different people—better, more heroic. Now the city was hungry and dusty. Young professionals and families were fleeing to the suburbs or even further, fleeing to bright, shiny places with names like California and Florida. The remaining people were depressed.

Officials threw event after event to raise morale: parades, circuses, fairs, motivational speeches, sporting competitions, bike races, hot-air balloon festivals. Everything worked, for a moment. People would fill the downtown, buy hot dogs and funnel cakes, and the city would burst with life. Then, everyone would go home. People in the suburbs would talk about what an experience they'd had, and the people in the city would thumb through Florida and California brochures, where they were sure people ate funnel cake every day.

One morning in 1949, after a carnival came to Centerville, the mayor and a city councilman were strolling through downtown, past abandoned skyscrapers and shuttered shop fronts. The wind flipped carnival rubbish down the street like industrial tumbleweeds.

"This isn't working," Ted, the mayor, said. He'd only been in office for nine months, and he couldn't sleep at night. "The problem is that all our solutions are temporary. Within a week, people have forgotten them. We need something permanent. What's the most permanent thing you can think of?"

His companion shrugged.

"I'll tell you what's really permanent," the mayor said to the councilman. "A castle. A castle can withstand almost anything."

The mayor had been an infantryman in Europe five years earlier. The first time he'd seen a castle, he was dumbstruck. People had stood on those walls 500 years ago, and the walls still stood, even amidst the destruction and squalor of war.

Now, his own city, less than one hundred years old, was falling apart. When his grandparents had immigrated to America from Germany in 1890, Centerville was the pride of the country. His grandfather and father had both worked in a factory, building locomotive engines, and they had done well.

But where other cities had managed to come back after the Great Depression, Centerville never did. It lost industries. It lost people. It lost hope. The tall, proud buildings were half-empty. The city was beginning to rust.

"We're going to build a castle," Ted told the councilman.

The councilman laughed. He thought it was a joke.

"I'm serious," Ted said. "I have a little boy, and I want him to be proud of something." Whether he meant the city or himself, the councilman couldn't tell.

This would be Ted's big gamble as mayor. Every year the people would attack that castle. A siege. It would provide a release valve for their aggression, and the castle would still be standing, a tangible symbol of their resilience.

It was a crazy idea. Maybe the city wouldn't have gone for it at any other time or if people hadn't still remembered the recent good times when the city was prosperous and happy; if they hadn't felt that everything else had been tried; if the mayor weren't so young, so sure, so passionate, so convincing. If all those things hadn't been true, perhaps the castle wouldn't have been built.

TED PUT THE CASTLE at the heart of the city, in a grand park no one visited anymore. Skyscrapers from the city's heyday ringed the park. The castle, in contrast, was a squat square with four towers and a gatehouse. It was utterly out of place. The castle was ancient, and the city was modern. The castle was stone, and the city was iron.

On June 22, 1951, the city held its first siege. Ted got into his car with his wife, Judy. Their son, Johnny, sat between them. Ted had been preparing for this moment for two years. He had mounted a huge PR campaign—mailings, newspaper ads, radio spots, and billboards—to get the city excited for the siege. Still, it was possible that no one would show up.

As they drove closer and closer to the city center, traffic moved slower and slower. Parked cars lined the streets for the last mile. Ted didn't remember downtown being this crowded since 4th of July fireworks when he was a child.

"Everyone came," Judy said to Ted.

She was right. No one wanted to miss out.

Ted, Judy, and Johnny joined the rest of the city officials on an observation platform. The officials were all milling about, terse and nervous.

By ten o'clock all the defenders had entered the castle, lining its battlements. The attackers formed a wide circle all around. The city gave the attackers tall and heavy ladders, ropes with grappling hooks, and a giant battering ram. The defenders were given grey beach balls and cauldrons of warm water that simulated rocks and boiling oil. As an attacker, if you were hit by either, you were supposed to move to the outskirts. Everyone had a belt with flags. If someone grabbed your flag, you were out. But the city had vastly overestimated people's ability to stay in control of their aggression. Almost as soon as the sirens announced the beginning of the siege, orderly play gave way to straight-out brawl.

In hindsight, it had been naïve to think that people would be able to rein in their passion. They had been angry for too long. Now, they were invited to a war. They snuck in rolls of quarters, brass knuckles, socks filled with pennies, pipes, baseball bats, stones, bricks, and sticks.

Even from a distance, Ted could tell that people had abandoned the script. The other city officials could see it too. They shifted from foot to foot. It was clear to everyone that something was going wrong.

A castle? How could they have been so stupid?

Ted stood unwavering, silent.

Judy fiddled with her clutch.

Johnny perched on Ted's shoulders for a better view.

After an hour, the sirens sounded again, signaling the end of the siege. Paramedics swept in to tend to injuries, far more than had been expected. Two people died—an attacker named Glen and a defender named Doris. The city officials felt sick. They could already imagine the lawsuits. They told Ted again and again that they had known this was an awful idea.

Ted heard a sound coming from inside the castle. It grew louder and louder. The city officials backed away nervously; they expected an irate mob. But as it rose, it became clear that the sound wasn't angry. There was cheering and singing. People streamed out of the castle, arm-in-arm, reveling like sports fans whose team had just won the championship.

People weren't disgusted by the violence and the deaths. They were energized. These people had been looking for a release. They had been so deep in their funk, so depressed for so long, that they hadn't realized how thirsty they were for something real. And what's more real than death? People immediately celebrated Doris and Glen. For decades, attackers would chant Glen's name and defenders would rally to cries of Doris. A fake siege wouldn't have worked, but the real thing left them elated. Bruised, hurt, aching, cut, and woozy—but elated.

People built fires in the streets, musicians fetched instruments, attackers shared bottles with defenders, and everyone danced. Ted and Judy walked Johnny through the celebrations. Wary police officers wandered around, but the violence was out of everyone's system. Ted and Judy drove their sleepy child home.

After tucking Johnny into bed, Ted and Judy sat on the edge of the bed.

"Buddy, you just saw the birth of something new and great," Ted said to his son. "We're not just going to save this city. We're going to make it the best city in the country."

Johnny smiled at him, sleepy and proud. Ted hadn't fully believed it before he saw the people reveling, but now he knew it was true. He was going to do something amazing.

BUT NOTHING CHANGED. For all the pleasure the people had taken in the siege, they still woke up poor and without jobs. Critics said this was just another stunt. Ted disagreed. The city just needed time.

The second and third sieges were more violent and more successful than the first, but things remained bleak. City officials complained. Nothing was changing.

Be patient, Ted told them. Cities don't turn around overnight. Things were changing. He pointed to the sharp decline in violent crime with sticks.

Then, one night in spring, Ted was walking around the block with Johnny. He stopped short at one house. Someone had pounded a For Sale sign into the front yard. Ted looked around. No house had sold on this street for over a decade.

A week later, the house sold. When the family moved in the father said—rather sheepishly—that they wanted to be part of the siege. No one who lived outside of the city limits could take part in the siege. This family had moved away to the suburbs ten years earlier and never once regretted it, until the siege began.

A month later, another sold. Then another. Soon all vacant houses were selling. Centerville had lost a quarter of its population over the past decade, and it regained most of that within the year. People wanted a piece of the siege. Pessimism dissipated like fog. Businesses moved back into the empty skyscrapers. People rented the high-rise apartments. New restaurants launched. Everyone who wanted a job had a job. Everyone who wanted a house had a house. Reporters flocked. Ted was a sensation. He was even featured on the cover of Time magazine, holding a shield and a sword.

The city was suddenly flush with taxes. Ted had money to play with. He invested in infrastructure and education. He built beautiful parks and modern schools. He planted trees along boulevards and gardens in lost corners. He hired new police, new firemen, new street sweepers, new gardeners, and new garbage collectors. He wanted to build a city that everyone wanted to live in.

The fourth, fifth, and sixth sieges were bigger and better than ever. More passionate. More people died, but once again, as soon as the siege was over, the tension drained from the city. Crime was almost unheard of. Ted was reelected for a third term by a 97% margin.

In 1957, THEY BUILT A NEW WALL in a wide circle around the old castle wall, to make room for all the new people. But that wasn't enough for Ted. He wanted this castle to be just like a real castle. Better. Money was abundant. So, he added a towering keep at the center of it all. He stacked level upon level, with courtroom, kitchens, dining rooms on the bottom floors, bedrooms and living areas above that, and, on the top floors, a library, game room, and movie theatre. At the very top was a small tower with an observatory. Ted loved nooks and surprises, so the architects added hidden doorways and secret passages throughout. The keep rose 164 feet, ornamented with gargoyles.

The keep was finished in 1960. The city wanted Ted, Judy, and Johnny to move into the castle. It had been built to be lived in, and who else could live there? Ted demurred, but was secretly thrilled. Judy wasn't so sure.

"I don't have nearly enough furniture," she said to her friends that evening over *mai tais*.

"You'll get new furniture," her friends said.

"Well, I certainly wouldn't mind an extra bedroom or ten," she laughed. "But don't expect me to dust."

Johnny, twelve now, was even more excited than Ted. How many boys get to live in a castle? So, it was settled. But even after moving in, Judy and Ted took pride in living the same Midwestern life. Judy shopped at the SuperValue and cooked roasts, meatloaf, and casseroles. They had friends over to play euchre on Saturdays and kept bowling in their Tuesday night league. Johnny went to the public schools and played football and baseball.

Ted was re-elected for his fourth term that year. People love a politician who stays true to his roots, even if he lives in a castle. Especially if he lives in a castle.

In 1963, THE CITY STARTED whispering about Vietnam. If people stopped to think about it, which they generally tried not to do, they found themselves feeling strange about participating in this mock war when a real war was raging on the other side of the world; but people enjoyed their siege too much, so most people ignored the war overseas.

In 1964, worried that Ted's fourth and final term as mayor was almost over, the people voted to replace the position of mayor with a position of king. No term limits. There was no law that a city needed a mayor. It was an outrageous idea, but then so was a castle. They were the only city in America with a castle; why couldn't they be the only city in America with a king?

"Ted loves his little castle," Judy said over a bridge hand, "but his being king won't change us."

Johnny still continued to live like an ordinary high school kid. If it was strange to live in a castle and be the son of the only king in America, he didn't show it. He was popular, but not the most popular. He was smart, but it didn't show in his grades. During his senior year, Johnny started dating Sally Johnson. She was head of the science club. For their first date, he invited her to look at stars from the castle's observatory. It was an exciting time to be looking at stars, because of the space race.

They got married in 1968 and pregnant the next year. Sally said it happened in July, when astronauts were landing on the moon. She teased Ted that she was going to name the child Moon; he fretted that people would think they were hippies.

Quite the opposite. When Johnny's number fell high in the draft lottery, he immediately enlisted. Sally complained that she was four months pregnant, but he pointed out that he was going to have to go either way. He shipped off to Vietnam in 1970 and sent cheerful letters that said conditions were worse than he could have imagined. Sally wrote back to say her belly was huge and her back hurt a lot. He wrote that the idea of their child kept him warm on rainy nights.

And then, while his squad was working its way through the jungle, he triggered a tripwire that set off an old French grenade. Judy and Sally cried for days when they heard he had died, and Ted stared dumbly from the walls of his castle. His boy. His sweet, strong boy.

Sally gave birth to a son a week later. She bore him into a sea of turbulent emotions. The birth was difficult. She was so numb from grief that she slept for two days and demonstrated no interest in the baby. She rolled over and showed her back to him, so the nurses handed the baby to Judy, instead. She and Ted held him for hours. When the nurse asked if they knew what name to put on the birth certificate, Ted told them Jonathan, Jr.

"That wasn't your choice to make, Ted," Judy told him after the nurse left.

"Sally would want to name him after his father," Ted said. "He was a great man." He wanted to say boy, not man. Johnny would always be a boy to him.

"Plus," he said, "it's better than Moon."

When she woke up. Sally shrugged.

"That's fine," she said and turned away. No, she didn't want to see the baby. She was tired. No, she couldn't breastfeed right now.

They brought Sally back to the castle after two days. She sat in her room. She held the baby when he was handed to her, but it looked to Ted like she felt she was holding someone else's baby.

"I don't get it," he said to Judy, while she was fixing some formula.

Judy thought about it. "Maybe people react in different ways to loss. Maybe there's some that cling to the baby because it's all they have left of the person, but there's also some that push the baby away, because it reminds them of what they've lost."

"That's ridiculous," Ted said. "It's her baby."

Judy filled a bottle.

At dinner the three of them sat around the table, mostly silent. Ted took to reading the evening newspaper. He read about planes hijacked by terrorists, riots at colleges, and the deaths of drugged-out rock stars. He read about the war. He read about hippies protesting the war. He read about hippies marching on the capital. He read about hippies blowing themselves up while making a bomb to protest the war. He tapped his foot with great agitation.

"These dirty hippies don't know how good they have it."

Judy smiled and nodded. Sally looked down at her food.

By the next year, the war protesters started protesting the siege as well as the war. Ted stood on top of the keep. He was holding Jack the same way he used to hold Johnny during the sieges. He growled about the damn peaceniks. It was bad enough that they were disrespecting the war effort, but his siege? He was saving the city. Go home hippies.

Sally looked down at the crowds. She said quietly, "I think it's good that they're protesting the war."

Ted stared at her like she was speaking Vietnamese.

She said, "If we had listened to them, Johnny would still be alive."

"What?"

Judy looked nervously between them.

"The war is meaningless, so his death is meaningless," Sally said.

Ted kicked over a TV table with a tray of drinks on it. The glasses shattered on the stone floor. "The hell it is. He was doing his duty."

"Vietnam is a joke. The politicians are playing a game. They're watching from afar," she said, motioning at the attackers massed below, "while all our men die for them."

Ted put his hands on the battlements. He tried to push his fingers through the rock. No one was sending anyone to die. They were securing freedom. They were securing prosperity.

He turned to Sally. For a minute he just looked into her eyes. She met his stare. His hand twitched. He almost raised it.

Finally, breathed out slowly.

"Get out of my castle," he said.

Sally turned and left Judy holding Jack. She went to her room, packed a few things into a backpack, and marched past the castle walls, past the protesters, past the attackers, out of the city.

Months later, she sent Judy a postcard. She was living on a commune in the northeast. She hoped Jack was doing okay, and she begged Ted to reconsider the siege.

He threw the card into the fireplace. How could she get it so wrong?

Neither the siege nor the war was about violence. He was as sad as anyone else that Johnny had died—it tore him up inside on a daily basis—but Johnny had to die so the rest of them could live normal, decent lives.

In 1975, after the end of the Vietnam War, the war protesters needed a new cause. They focused on Ted's siege. Every year, they came out in greater and greater numbers. Ted gritted his teeth and tried to disregard it all. If he ignored them long enough, perhaps they would go away.

FOR A FEW YEARS, Ted, Judy, and Jack got along well. Ted and Judy felt too old to be parents, but Jack was such an easy boy. He was quiet and solitary, and he enjoyed the company of his grandparents. But then, in 1977, Judy saw a doctor for a persistent cough and was diagnosed with cancer. Three months later, she died.

Her death left Ted wide-eyed. Not only was his companion gone, but he didn't know how to do basic things like shopping for groceries, cooking dinner, or balancing the checkbook. He bought cases of canned soup, canned vegetables, and boxed mac and cheese.

For a while, Ted kept going to euchre and bowling, but he felt his friends pitied him. So, he began to stay at home with Jack. Jack loved eating canned soup and TV dinners with his grandfather. They did puzzles. They read books. They explored the secret passages of the castle and often ate their dinners, picnic-style, in hidden rooms where they couldn't be found by the castle's staff. Ted would tell Jack his plans for the city. He still had big ideas. He was thinking about building a wall around the entire city, so that it would be like a medieval walled city.

Jack ate a bite of cream-of-mushroom soup and nodded. He was okay with walls. He only ever felt entirely safe inside the castle. His father and grandmother had died, and his mother had abandoned him. At school, the kids called him the Little Prince. Some of his classmates said that the siege was bad. The kids who hated it occasionally pushed and spit on him.

But things escalated on the day before the 30th siege. Four boys were pushing Jack around in the schoolyard. At this point, Ted had been king for 16 years.

"Your grandpa makes people fight each other. You like that?" a boy said. He punched Jack in the eye.

Jack dropped to the ground. For a second, Jack found it humorous that the boy had hit him in protest of fighting. Then, the boy kicked him in the stomach, and another boy kicked him in the face. Then, they were all kicking him.

He woke up in the nurse's office. Ted came bursting in. He hugged Jack fiercely. Jack winced. Ted was furious. He wanted the bullies expelled. But when Jack told him that they'd beaten him up in protest of the siege, Ted became silent. He drove Jack home with a white-knuckle grip on the wheel. He put Jack to bed and heated up some canned chicken noodle soup.

"Relax. You'll stay home from school the rest of the week. We'll watch movies together. F— those bullies."

He had a plan. He put in a phone call to the commanders of the siege, both the attackers and the defenders. He also called the police chief. These were people who still loved the siege, who distrusted protesters, who wanted things to go back to the way they had been. They wanted to feel the pride, the anger, the importance they'd felt the first time they'd participated in the siege.

The next day was the 30th siege. Ted used to find joy in watching all the city's people take their positions and surge forward, but today, he was just tired. He sat on the top of the keep with Jack next to him.

There were more protesters than ever this year. They linked arms and encircled the entire castle. They blocked the attackers from getting through. The siege began, but no one knew what to do. Some attackers squeezed through, but most of them milled around outside the castle, unable to bring the ladders and siege equipment through.

Ted patted Jack on the shoulder. "I'll be right back."

He walked down the stairs, out of the keep, and to the castle's gatehouse. He signaled the leaders of the defenders.

Then, he opened the gates of the castle. The protesters were chanting and singing, but as Ted walked out of the castle towards them, a hush rippled through them.

"Why are you doing this?" he yelled.

No one answered.

"Why are you doing this?" he repeated. "This siege is the only reason this city is great!"

A man stepped forward. He was young, but he had a beard that made him look older. He wore an army jacket. When he spoke, he wasn't loud.

"I just got back from Vietnam."

"I was in the army too. You're not the only one."

The man looked tired and sad. "Why would you want a pretend war?"

"War is painful, yes, but it's where we distinguish ourselves."

The young man shook his head. "This isn't glory. We're losing our humanity."

"No, this is us at our most majestic. Striving. Pushing. Conquering. Victorious."

"Murderous. Enraged. Greedy."

Ted closed his eyes. These kids didn't get it. They would never get it.

"Please," he said. "Please just go. This is your last chance."

The man laughed at him. Ted thought of the kids pummeling Jack. He turned and walked back into the castle.

All of the defenders had pulled off of the ramparts. It looked like they were giving up. But when Ted was inside the gates, the defenders did what they'd never done in thirty years. They sallied forth. They had always defended the walls, but now they charged out. They charged out and slammed into the surprised protesters.

Then, the attackers joined in. The police stood.

Ted walked up to the top of the keep, took Jack's hand, and led him down into one of their secret rooms. He had moved two cots in there, stacks of canned food, gallons of water, books for himself and comic books for Jack. There was a hot pad to cook on and a passageway that took them right to a bathroom. A couple of battery-run lanterns lit up the room. Jack was excited by the adventure of hiding away.

The peace protesters were entirely unprepared for the attack. They were trapped. The attackers and defenders—the people who loved the siege—lost control. They beat the protesters until they fell down and were still. The police finally stepped in, but by then hundreds of people needed ambulances. There were broken bones, concussions, and bleeding. One man lost an eye. One woman slipped into a coma. The remaining peace protesters fled. Everyone else milled about. Once the adrenaline wore off, they were left wondering what the hell they'd just done. Some people had no qualms about what had just happened, but most people felt uneasy. It was one thing when there were attackers and defenders.

But attackers and innocents? It wasn't the same. Some wondered what the hell they'd been doing for thirty years. They filtered away from the castle, slowly. They found their family members and drove home without speaking.

That was the last siege. Some people still wanted it, but most people were done. In addition, the king was missing. The siege quietly died.

Ted and Jack stayed hidden for a month. Ted wanted to escape notice for a while. He didn't want to be around for the aftermath. After the month was up, he took Jack's hand and walked right out of the castle. They walked through the park and down the street past the skyscrapers. It was Saturday. No one was around. The city was quiet.

They walked further and further out into the city, until they reached a motel. The attendant barely looked up, as Ted checked in and paid with cash. After a week, Ted found a small house to rent, just outside of the city. He didn't take anything from the castle. He bought new clothes, new furniture, and new toys for Jack. He left behind everything of Judy's and everything of Johnny's, every photograph and every memory.

Ted thought people would look for him, but nobody did. Maybe no one noticed he was gone. The city was just fine without him. No one was looking for him, angry about the attack on the protesters. No one was looking for him, desperate for him to save the day. No one.

They elected a new mayor and abandoned the siege, and still the city continued. People were happy. People were unhappy. They were fine.

The city was a good city. The city was a bad city. The city was a city.

And Ted just sat back and watched. He wrote letters to the U.S. government about Agent Orange. He sat on the porch. He was unimportant, and he was happy being unimportant.

He made mac and cheese, opened cans of soup, and took care of his grandson who loved him. He was happy.

Tejan Green

FOREIGN EXCHANGE

You ask me how I name things,
make sense of the uncanny.

A childhood whisper. Flesh and feather
brought home to roost, again.

Will you be content as a wife,
or do I have to call you lover—

Figuring a less passive path,
a thing more substantial.

And who are you anyway—you who were raised elsewhere,
but still manage to be so very here.

Silence. There is some relief in willful ignorance. Sap licked,
sucked dry. Still no satisfaction. The ruin settles
in the hum. We are present in the unwillingness to name things,
defiant. As if naming wasn't only an illusion,

a road beaten through virgin snow
while the sky remains open,

and we could make a thing whole by saying it so.
Dress it up so it is less naked.

You feign wholeness.
The wheels turn as you manufacture the lie,
pour years into it.

A beast
given
feminine
persona;
ridden hard,
put away
wet.

Claudia Hinz

BLESSINGS

OUR RABBI GIVES US a homework assignment. It is a challenge he probably thought carefully about assigning, knowing he might not see us again for a while. Not that our congregation is loosey-goosey, but we are prone to skip Saturday Torah service and Sunday School when there is fresh snow on the mountain. Many of us might not return until the High Holidays, when our deeply entrenched, genetically-encoded obligation (call it guilt) drives us back to *shul*. Every week, as the faces before him change, our rabbi asks if we've done our homework.

"When was the last time you blessed someone?"

We look around sheepishly.

"Not a partner or your best friend, but someone you don't know. Someone you just met, or the grocery store clerk you see every week, a person on the street, anyone in need of a blessing."

No one raises a hand.

"Turn to the person next to you," he instructs us. "This is how the blessing works. You face the person, look into his or her eyes, then—and here's the crux of it—you don't think. You open yourself to channeling the blessing that person needs. You begin by saying, 'I want to bless you.' "

I want to bless you. These words make us uncomfortable. They are at best presumptuous, at worst hubristic. *Cheesy*, my children would say.

Who am I to bless? Isn't that what we ask God to do in the quiet of the Amidah prayer on Shabbat, tented under our prayer shawls, seeking a private audience with Hashem, offering our hotly whispered prayers that we might somehow, miraculously, be heard?

I am paired with a good friend. We both realize this is cheating, but we don't offer to switch with other people in our row. I am already deliberating the blessing I know she needs after weeks of worrying about her daughter, a college student far away. It occurs to me that I might tell her exactly what I need, really expedite the whole blessing thing, maybe even improve my chances for receiving.

It is awkward to stare into her eyes, which I note for the first time in our twenty-year friendship are gorgeous, a velvety chocolate color. After we exchange blessings, we hug each other. I know we didn't do it right. Our blessings were cardboard, stiff and rehearsed.

As if he knows this, our rabbi says, "Keep practicing. You don't get good overnight."

Somebody has the nerve to ask, "What if someone doesn't want to be blessed. By us." She means us as Jews. "What if they take it the wrong way?" She means like we're trying to convert them.

"You'd be surprised," the rabbi says. "Try it, and let me know how it goes. Email me."

We sing Shalom Aleychem, a prayer in which the Hebrew is so close to the Arabic version that I always hear the companion words, a mere vowel or two off. We sing of ministering angels who trail us home on Shabbat. I imagine I hear the whisper of angels' wings, as I head out into the cold night. I drive slowly, so I don't lose them. I think of the angels pinching my coat tails with wispy angel fingers, sweeping with a gust into my home. I wonder what I need to say or do to keep them here with us, a presence I might feel always.

When I remember, I try to bless. I try not to deliberate or word the blessing in my head, before I offer it. I cannot pretend the blessing is spontaneous, when it isn't.

In an Uber ride to the airport, my older daughter and I get into a conversation with the driver about his work in his church. He asks about my life and what I plan to do, now that I am an empty nester. He asks my daughter about her pre-med studies, her desire to become a surgeon and help people through the worst diagnoses. When he pulls up to the curb at the airport, he shifts the car gears into park and turns around. For the first time in our forty-minute ride, I look into his face. He is much younger than I am. I imagine him returning home and squatting to hug his small children, greeting his wife who also works two jobs.

"Would it be okay if I prayed for you?" he asks.

"Yes," I say. I'm nervous. Will I be asked to speak to his Father? Accept his Jesus as my savior?

He uses our names in his prayer, except that he reverses them. His prayer for my daughter is addressed to me, and mine to her, so it comes out that I might work hard to complete my studies and become a healing doctor, and my daughter might write books that open people's eyes to how everyone is hurting and how we might heal one another.

In the middle of his prayer, my daughter and I simultaneously peek at each other and smile at the mixed-up names, our identities crossed, our fates switched. Then, we again bow our heads respectfully.

When he is finished, I say, "Now I'd like to bless you."

"Yeah?" he says. "Cool."

"I'm Jewish, so I'll begin with the Hebrew introduction to prayer."

"No way, man. You speak Hebrew?"

He shifts in his seat, like he's settling in, and he closes his eyes. He looks much more relaxed than I feel.

"Baruch Hashem," I begin in the traditional way, acknowledging our God and the blessings in my life, before I do 'the ask'. I pray that this man will continue to serve families who need his help, that he will have the passion and energy for this important work and continue to feel gratified by it. I pray that his family will be healthy and that each of them will experience great joy and love.

He is nodding. Every once in a while, he calls out, "Amen."

When I am done, he shakes our hands.

That was a year ago. His were not the blessings we needed, as it turns out. I wonder now, twelve months nearly to the day, if I prayed for what he really needed, if his family is healthy, if he is still finding satisfaction in his work and managing to work two jobs. How could I possibly know what he needed? How could he know what I would need? We were strangers.

Here is what I am learning about the act of blessing. On some level, you have to gauge whether a person will be okay with the intimate moment he or she hasn't asked for. I have walked away from more than a few people feeling the blessing didn't go so well. It's easier to bless someone whose injury is obvious, someone with a cast or crutches. "I want to bless you with a swift and complete recovery." This is generally well received, and it sounds more sincere than saying, "Get better soon."

Why is that? I wonder. Is it because there is an intention, an implied participation, perhaps even an absurd implication that I might somehow, miraculously have a direct line to Hashem? It feels like the blessing should overcome me, like a moment of unconsciousness, when I just blurt it out. This might feel like truly channeling something, like those rare moments in writing when I'm in the zone, madly, furiously scribbling as if taking dictation, inscribing words that come from outside of me, so that later, I can barely make out what I've written.

Today, I'm in the grocery store. I have a cart load of groceries, weird stuff I don't usually buy, items for my husband who has just had surgery. Aspirin to prevent blood clots and water bottles to freeze for an ice machine contraption attached to his leg. Flowers. I'm rushing to get back to him, so he's not tempted to get up from the couch and hobble on his own to the kitchen.

I hurry through the check-out line, fighting the urge to offer to pack my own bags, because I don't want to offend the checker. After paying, I hustle out, and because I'm dead-tired, I head to the Starbucks counter. A man with a long ponytail takes a step back, when I zoom up.

"Oh, sorry," I say. "I didn't mean to cut."

He waves his hand. "No, no," he says. "You go ahead. I have all the time in the world."

I debate moving aside, but there is my full, unwieldy cart with so much stuff. I'm suddenly embarrassed, as if he can see I am going home to a big, empty house. If I move the cart behind him, I will be blocking the way of other shoppers with carts. I bow my head. The roses I have chosen are pale pink, the petals edged in green, like a prematurely picked fruit. It occurs to me that the roses have been dyed, and I feel tricked.

When it is my turn to order, I ask the man with the ponytail what he's having, and I pay for his drink.

"That's very nice of you," he says.

I thank him for letting me go ahead of him.

"Just basic courtesy," he says. "Easy."

It's awkward standing there with him, waiting for our drinks which are both under my name, as if we're together. I check my phone for text messages, so that I don't have to look at him.

"Might I ask your name?" he says. His enunciation is vaguely old-fashioned and formal. We are standing three feet apart. I can't pretend not to see him. There is something of the creative, free spirit in his mellow demeanor, his long, groovy ponytail.

"I'm Claudia."

"Nice to meet you, Claudia. I'm Angel."

"Angel? That's a beautiful name."

"As is Claudia."

We shake hands.

"Angel," I repeat. And then without thinking, I say. "May you be an angel to everyone around you."

He closes his eyes and nods slowly. For a second, I think I have made him sad. "I try," he says.

"And..." I'm on a roll. "May you find yourself surrounded by angels at every turn." I hear my voice crack. An ache rises from my chest to block my throat. Do I tell him I have been waiting for an angel? That my people are hurting, and I can't take their pain away?

"Thank you," he says, accepting the white mocha from the *barista*. Angel turns back to me. "You have a grateful day now," he says. Then, he turns and walks away.

A grateful day. I repeat this in my head. Maybe, this is Angel's signature greeting. Maybe, his hippie friends tease him and ask to see his healing crystals. He didn't start by saying, "I want to bless you," so maybe, it wasn't a blessing. Just a goodbye.

I watch him saunter off, slowly. All the time in the world. I don't know that I have ever in my life sauntered so slowly. His pant legs drag on the ground, trampled by his heels and crusted with snow. I'm suddenly curious about his shoes. What shoes has Angel chosen for this particular errand?

Grateful. My husband is safely out of surgery.

My child is in pain, though. I cannot do anything to help, even as she knows I stand by, eager to try. My love does not feel like anything close to enough. But she is loved, and I am loved. Wildly, wildly loved.

My husband will heal. Not today or tomorrow. But he will heal. Eventually, we might all heal.

A petal falls into my hand, the pinky sunrise of the rose splattered by the foam of my latte. The petal is drenched, but it is silky and too beautiful to drop into the garbage. I cup it in my palm, hold it high above the concrete, as I bump my shopping cart through the parking lot. In my hand, the sun rises on a new day.

Lidia Kosk
Danuta E. Kosk-Kosicka, Translator

RETURN

Look—

A cormorant
like the one that flew over
our heads back then

We were so lofty
the earth under our feet
wings fluttering above us

Lidia Kosk
Danuta E. Kosk-Kosicka, Translator

ON THE TRAIL

I did not meet you
on the Tatra mountain trail

but found your presence while
climbing steep ridges

You were here
You showed that every path could be

walked to the end
victory on a human scale

mountains and space
contemplation and deeds

stumbles
stones sliding down

The last word need not be spoken
to be heard

Andrew Lafleche

THE LIFE AND DEATH OF ARTHUR MILLER

FOURTEEN DAYS AFTER Arthur Miller's sixteenth birthday, both his parents were killed in an automobile accident when a drunken driver swerved into their lane, as they returned home from a night at the theater. Their deaths occurred instantly, and to that effect, neither were able to be viewed with an open coffin at their post-life nuptials. The last time Arthur saw his parents alive was in the moments following Sunday dinner. His mother in a dress, glowing. His father dressed handsomely, saying, "When you finally meet the woman who makes the world stand still, Son, don't ever quit doing for her what you did at the start. That way there will never be an end."

Arthur clung to these words in the weeks that followed. He clung to everything his father had said, for his father was the wisest person Arthur had ever known. The only compromise Arthur made, knowing his father wouldn't approve, was that immediately following the funeral, Arthur dropped out of school. Postponing his education was the rationalization. He took up work at the local textile mill in order to afford residence in the house his parents had raised him in; to cover the cost of the burial; to pay for all the costs of living he had never known as a child, for his father had always provided. There was the phone bill, though only solicitors ever called. The electric company had to be paid, as did the taxes to the town and the oil for the furnace. He had to buy food for the table and the occasional article of clothing. The expenses were not great. He was alone after all, but as any sixteen-year-old forced to earn his way in the world can attest, it was not easy.

After several months, Arthur settled into his new normal, rising with the sun during the summer months and before the sun in winter, grabbing his lunch pail which he prepared the evening prior, and walking to his post at the mill. During the summer, he finished in time to observe the sun set, as he walked home to prepare his lunch for the following day. In the winter, it was as dark as when he left for work in the morning. Day in, day out, Arthur became accustomed to the grind of existence.

In time, he was able to save enough money to purchase his first vehicle, a practical blue Chevrolet Caprice Classic, and he taught himself to drive. Outsiders thought his choice morbid, as it was the same model car his parents had been killed in, but Arthur didn't think so. He found two rubber bands and secured a picture of his parents to the visor above the driver's seat. Every time he sat behind the steering wheel, he was reminded to treat the privilege of driving most seriously. And he did.

Arthur always drove with his hands at ten and two on the wheel. He checked his mirrors at regular intervals and physically turned to observe his blind spots, whenever he changed lanes. The one thing he never did was drink and drive. In fact, Arthur never touched a drop of alcohol. He wasn't a prude about it. He wasn't an evangelist of abstinence. He simply did not perceive any benefits to ingesting the liquid, and knew all too well, the devastating consequences.

Some year later, as a young adult, mobile and employed, Arthur decided it was time to complete his high school education. He enrolled in a weekend program at the community college in the next town over. Monday to Friday, he labored at the mill; on Saturday and Sunday, he attended classes. He did not mind the lengthening of his already long weeks. In fact, Arthur rather enjoyed the new endeavor. Early on in the program, he developed an affection for his instructor, Ms. Annabelle Hastings, a conservative woman who was only four years his senior. Her hair was golden as the fall harvest; her eyes as miraculous as the green flash of a perfect sunset. Nevertheless, he was the son of his father. He did not act on his longings, until he obtained his diploma.

When he finished his education a full year later, he wasted no time in establishing a courtship with, then proposing to, and quickly marrying the woman who stood his world still. Their journey together was a fairy tale, and keeping with his father's example, he treated her as his queen. Every Sunday Arthur would buy fresh flowers and, in the evening after dinner, he would take her on a romantic date. He continued to do so, even after Annabelle birthed their first and only son, Henry. If you continue to do the things you did at the start of the relationship, there will never be an end.

By all appearances, the Miller's were a model family, right down to the white picket fence. When Henry was old enough to attend school, Annabelle returned to her own classroom. Arthur accepted a promotion as the manager of the mill. The job guaranteed each weekend free to spend with his family. They wanted for nothing.

Henry excelled in mathematics, while also demonstrating superb athletic capabilities. He captained every scholastic team he played on and was respected by his peers. Like his father, he stayed away from intoxicants, and he held a deep civic responsibility. Upon graduating high school, Henry enlisted with the 82nd All Americans and moved to Fort Bragg. There, he was readied for deployment to Iraq.

Both of his parents were extremely proud, and although Arthur did not display the 'My son is an Honor Student and Serviceman' bumper sticker he'd secretly purchased at the recruitment office, he did keep it bound to the visor beside his parent's fading picture.

During this time, Annabelle's doctor discovered a concerning lump in her breast and referred her to a specialist. Under compassionate authority, Henry's deployment was deferred, until his mother's biopsy results were returned. Fortunately, the results were negative, the tumor was benign, and all was well. With these worries relieved, Henry deployed to Iraq for his first tour of duty.

Near the end of his experience, while on patrol outside Baghdad, Henry's section was ambushed. Henry caught a piece of shrapnel in the back of his head. He returned in a flag-draped coffin.

Needless to say, Arthur and Annabelle were devastated, spirit void, ghosts. Arthur, while fraught with re-imaginings of his parent's murder and now his son's—for Annabelle's sake—remained the cornerstone of their mourning marriage.

Annabelle took leave from teaching, for she was too distraught to be around children who would grow into the noble young adults that her Henry never would. She remained at home mostly, too burdened to do much of anything. Soon, that benign lump was benign no longer. The doctors decided that it had been cancerous from the start. Now, it had metastasized in her lungs and heart and most of her chest.

Within six months, she died.

Inside of a year, Arthur had lost Henry and Annabelle, both of them his pride and joy. He was suddenly alone.

After the funeral, he requested a two-week leave of absence from the mill in order to collect himself. He assured the owners that he would return fully prepared to fulfill his duties without distraction. Arthur had not requested a day off, nor had he been sick, from he day he first set foot inside the textile mill at age sixteen.

The owners granted his request, and as Arthur had assured them, when he returned, he was renewed and composed once again. The owners, however, during the time Arthur spent recovering, had filled his position with a college graduate who was better qualified and came at a lesser salary. Upon his return, Arthur was given two weeks severance and dismissed with a handshake.

He drove home in a daze, his mind completely consumed with the utter unfairness of being let go. The daze became anger, then wheeled into bargaining, which led to depression, and by the time he'd accepted his dismissal, a horn blared. Arthur swerved to right himself in his lane. He pulled over immediately, hands gripping the steering wheel, his jaw clenched. Arthur inhaled and let it go, blowing all the air out. He turned off the ignition, unbuckled his seatbelt, and checked over his shoulder before opening the door. He thumbed the lock-knob to secure the car and started the familiar walk home.

He retired to his bedroom, sat on his side of the bed, and sighed. With no one left to be strong for, Arthur allowed himself to cry.

So overdrawn were his tears that his eyes swelled and stung with release. He cried with his face in his hands, tears burning down his wrists and to his elbows which soaked two circles on his trousers. His chest heaved, as the losses rushed forth. Arthur cried, until he could cry no more. Then, he rubbed his face and smoothed his cheeks. He bit his knuckle, as he rested his chin on his clasped hands. Outside, it was getting dark. He sat on his bed, thinking. He decided to sit still, until he knew what to do.

As the sun set, he concluded that, in the morning, he would pick up a newspaper and start looking for a new job.

He hummed his approval and stood to carry out his ablutions before bed. Maybe it was the sudden rush with which he stood, or perhaps his legs were asleep having sat so long. Whatever the reason, Arthur lost his balance. His skull connected with a corner of the dresser and then with the hardwood floor. There, he died in a puddle of his own blood and tears.

Linda Lamenza

POEM WITH NO REGRET

This is the one with blooming
irises and beebalm behind
the rocks, between the moss patches.
The one where I am content
on the patio, facing the woods,
all my plants carefully selected
and growing with no interference.
There is no unpublished book or
unborn child. No failed orchestral
musician or marine biologist.
No time not spent with
aging parents and young children.
Or endless hours of handwringing.
Nothing about wishing I had learned
to knit or to skydive.
No hours spent revising, recreating
this poem into something it is not.
There is not one thought
of what this could have been.

Xiaoly Li

MY MOTHER'S STORY

I ran away from home
to join the revolution, at sixteen.
Now my parents are
the sacrifice on the altar.
My father shot dead in jail,
the county education head
of the old government.
My mother drowned
herself in the well.
Years and years, a journey
spent searching for home.

Like the day when
betrayal announced
I was a Rightist,
enemy of the Republic.
Blood lost its warmth,
muscles couldn't move the bones.
Gasping, I uttered no words.
Following the liberation army
across the homeland and afar,
I saved the wounded in
most hard-fought wars.
At the forced-labor camp,
those sleepless nights, I asked why.

Catherine Lieuwen

WHAT OUR DREAMS TRY TO TELL US

IN THE FIRST DREAM I HAD, I tested positive for coronavirus. Delirious, I woke up and fell to my knees, praying. I recall saying, "No, no, no . . ." over and over again.

Subsequent nights included dreams in which I was repeatedly trying to call my doctor but getting a "wrong number" or "out of business" message. I dreamt about people in HAZMAT suits chasing me, and I had suffocation dreams.

I have no doubt that, as COVID-19 becomes the new zeitgeist of our time, my dreams and nightmares are a byproduct of streaming too many virus movies, watching too much news and doing too many web searches starting with "coronavirus and _____."

Last night was the most horrific nightmare by far.

In my dream, I had to take an emergency flight out of LAX to see an old boyfriend. We had recently reconnected over social media because of the pandemic, and we both agreed that we still loved each other and wanted to be together.

As some small shred of compassion was still left in the apocalyptic pandemic world, the government was issuing each citizen a one-way "final flight" to meet up with a loved one.

We were told that this was the last chance we had to see each other again, as global tourism was shutting down—for good. Once we reached our destination, we could never travel again.

When I entered the airport, I was shocked by what I saw.

The airport was packed as frantic travelers pushed and shoved and trampled each other to reach their last allotted flight, before the borders would be sealed. The world was hours away from a full and permanent lockdown.

All tourists wore gloves and masks. Many had strange, makeshift protective gear—from snorkeling masks to duct-tape-and-plastic-bag body suits that almost looked like body bags. Employees were covered from head to toe with gas masks and major protective gear.

Horrified, I turned around to leave but was abruptly stopped by two security agents in biohazard gear. I was told firmly that there was "no turning back."

I watched the glass doors to the outside seal shut with a sickening, vacuum-like swoop.

As they pushed me with rifles toward the TSA line, I fished through my purse for my passport and government papers, which included more personal information than I had ever given anyone.

I carried some kind of special passport—something I had applied for that let me travel one last time to be with—and quite possibly die with—the one I loved.

The passports were given out by a lottery system, and my number had recently been chosen by the government.

Now, airport employees were yelling over megaphones. The National Guard was deployed inside and outside the building. Police and police dogs were everywhere.

The TSA was stretched to its breaking point, like ropes on a breaking bridge over a deadly river.

As I set my bags down on the security belt, I was told to strip down to my bra and underwear. Before I would protest, a security officer handed me a towel, and two women in PPE lead me to a decontamination shower. There, they passed me a white paper gown and told me to take off my bra and underwear.

(This is quite possibly a memory of a real-life trauma I experienced in my college sorority when I was, along with the other new pledges, awakened in the night, led to shower, told to strip and remove all jewelry and nail polish. We were given white sheets to cover ourselves, until we were taken to an undisclosed location for a clandestine ceremony—about a topic so secret that if we told a soul, our lips would "wither and return to dust." Perhaps another piece on this true story later.)

In the dreamt airport bathroom, I stepped into a narrow, plexiglass decontamination chamber and held out my arms, as a cold, chlorine mist sprayed over my shivering body.

I put on the paper gown and was then escorted by a woman to more TSA checkpoints—a kind of X-Ray scanner like the TSA has now that can see through your clothes. Instead of scanning for the typical terrorist weapons like knives, bombs, and guns, though, this one was scanning for bioweapons.

Even though I had nothing on but a paper gown, I kept beeping. I had to go through the scanner several times.

I finally made it through the machine after a long line and was given a green hospital bracelet. I was then told that my belongings, clothes and luggage would be returned to me once I was seated on the plane. All I had was my gown, plastic coverings on my feet, and my plane ticket.

On my way to the gate, I was looking around, so horrified and bewildered at what I saw that I lost my footing going up the escalator and tripped. I fell and cut my palm open on one of the jagged, metal stairs. As I struggled to rise at the top of the escalator, a policewoman, a high-ranking male police officer, and some kind of high-security airport agent surrounded me and lifted me to my feet.

The gash on my palm was bright red and bleeding. A woman in a HAZMAT suit took out a scanner that resembled those forehead temperature scanners we've become all too accustomed to lately.

"I don't have a fever!" I said, "They took my temperature when I got here. "

"We're not scanning for fever, Ma'am," the high-security police officer said, "We're scanning your blood for bioterrorism."

"What?"

The woman scanned the cut on my palm.

As we waited for the results on the scanner, the police officer said, "Ma'am, you understand that if you test positive, you will be 100% guilty of international terrorism."

I began to gasp for air. I wasn't sure if this was from the shock of what I had just heard, or if I was suddenly experiencing a telltale symptom of the virus. One of the officers readied his gun, and another slapped a handcuff on my wrist. Then, I woke up.

Here I was in sweats, sitting up and panting.

As is often the case when waking up from a vivid nightmare, I was still groggy, trying to convince myself that the reality I was now back in did not contain elements of my staggeringly frightening dream. I was scared.

I felt my forehead—cool to the touch. I turned on the light, got up, splashed cold water on my face, then found a clean towel instead of the used one in the bathroom. I wiped off my face and the sweat from the dream, washed my hands vigorously with orange liquid antibacterial soap, then used the clean towel to turn off the water and turn the doorknob.

I gulped some clean water from the glass on my nightstand and got back into bed. I didn't go back to sleep after that. I didn't dare.

In an April 5th, 2020 article in *USA Today* by Alia A. Dastagir entitled "Coronavirus Interrupted Our Lives: Now It's Infiltrating Our Dreams," Dastagir writes, "Experts say dreams are a way for people to understand themselves. Their main function is to process emotions, which for many people have been more intense during the pandemic. People's waking lives are fraught—fear, uncertainty, and helplessness pervade the day. Those same emotions make respite at night elusive."

She quotes psychologist Ian Wallace, who says, "In our lives… we're only consciously aware of about 2% of what's going on around us and the other 98% is subconscious. Most of that is emotional, and we use our dreams as a way of understanding those emotions…In a situation like this pandemic, where emotions are heightened, people's awareness of their dreams are also heightened and these dreams might seem more vivid and more scary."

Perhaps, in our waking lives, we can use our dreams as insights into our inner selves, as well as the hearts and minds of those dear to us. Coronavirus dreams are scary, but if we can use them as an opportunity rather than something to fear, we can connect with ourselves and others in a way that could lead to a more compassionate, healed, post-pandemic society.

I document my dreams here and elsewhere, hoping that this will be the case.

Jack Brendan Miller

FOR ISABEL NO. 2

Anywhere now, I have never been to Minnesota
Your eyes, they have their stillness
pale blue snow-like falling, that which descends far
or which I cannot reach because somehow they are too close

I dig out the flaming sword of Eden where we now near the ocean
though we are cast out of Paradise and there is no return,
your fingers reach through the night
(grasping the wet earth, the sand) touching the water

and if your goal be to reach that garden,
then close the gates (forever), and my body will disappear in
to the night time of San Francisco,
like the grass in Minnesota, when now there is
the ice sleeting over the mailbox where you write, (lovely)

Nothing in this city is or can wholly be and know
the beauty of the flame, the ocean, the light of the city which
forces me with the color of its contours
far apart and awaiting Death, that fruit of time

(I do not understand) how you long for Paradise,
digging the sword out, how the gate closes
and opens; but a lonely something knows within me:
The snowy blizzard of your eyes fools nobody

Edward Lee

CROSSES

Megan McGibney

STANDING OUTSIDE THE CHURCH

There were
threats of hell
drilled into
my young mind.

There were
priests, careless
during Confession
when I needed them most.

There were
hateful attitudes
toward the LGBT
and women being priests.

There were
blind eyes turned
toward the years of
rape and abuse.

But there were also
the art
the ashes
the saints
the rosary
the rituals
the Blessed Virgin
and her Beloved Son,

who stands with
me now,
standing outside,
looking in.

N. Minnick

MURIEL RUKEYSER

The agony of saying : the agony of not saying.
To sweat and to dream : to answer for the land for love for song.

Sit with me in consequential and lonely hours
where nothing fades from memory : the bird song,
the distant drone of traffic (always in back of this soundtrack),
a wind chime (I could take it down, but won't).

This landscape of possibilities : forsaken : this fern-laden
darkness-strewn landscape where proletariats and outcasts
pass each other unrecognized.

The present is poverty.
The past, safely, is none the worse for wear.
The future depends—always depends—on my unfinished spirit.

I, too, was born in a time of war.
My bones move within my flesh—I can feel them sometimes.

Sometimes they ache.

The bird is not singing : it is warning of a backyard predator.
Music and meaning, you say, are the same.

N. *Minnick*

SAY IT

The Hopi word is *sipala*,
which requires little articulation
and no teeth. It is almost a whisper
as is the Hindu *shantih*, the Persian *sula*,
the English *peace*.

Marlon Hacla
Kristine Ong Muslim, Translator

MELISMAS (SELECTED EXCERPTS)

From the latest sins, the perceived worth
of time spent on the disappearance of the body
is always filled with lies.
There is still a higher purpose for celestial
disabilities such as these. Each one decorates
yet again his own cage. Where do we
seek refuge? In the catalogued gods, at the back
of chapels, in the warehouse of saints?
Our plan has been to use a deep-sea dragnet, but the beach is still
over-run by those who are busily retrieving clothes . . .

What exactly is it that you
want? Monks, butterflies, licenses
to view twice your own
salvation from a different angle? Sort out
first the part of the body where gushing
blood ensues. Houses made of cotton, pillars
made of cotton, weaponry made of cotton
are what we have left here. Even the news
changes when traveling across the sea.
Even the perspective of enemies, who can
overtake us to bear out
the smoldering part of the farmland where their
happiness is grown, to peek at the last page
of the manuscript of their soul.

Tower over me, a blaze beneath your gaze
if that is what you want. I will call
to God while you are still not weeping . . .

Oh, copulating horses! If only
I have enough interest, I will buy
shawls in bulk, because evening is prettier
when shrouded. Morning is more mysterious
when there are naked bodies.
While fireflies are engrossed in sustaining their flickering glow,
everyone else incessantly brings the moment to a standstill.

Ayaz Daryl Nielsen

UNTITLED

rowing our night boats
toward the threshold
of an awakening
each stroke of the oars
immersed in forgiveness

Ayaz Daryl Nielsen

SAND HILLS

as twilight finds my chest
white sand, wetlands, and
rolling green hills beckon
walking among memories
of grandfather's homestead,
a catalogue of ranch-land,
hay, cattle, horses and
everyday interactions, of
relatives and memories
that sing . . . and, yes,
I will come, I will come
crossing my old and
worn boundaries,
exhaling peace

Sarah Odishoo

AN ALTAR AT THE THREE CROSSROADS

Context is more important than content.
> —Noam Chomsky

I LEARNED TO READ when I was two years old. I lived in an apartment with my parents, and across the hallway lived a family with two girls, ages eight and five. They both went to school, and when they came home, they would knock on my door and ask me to play school. They had a little table, two little chairs, and a chalkboard in their hallway. The five-year-old and I would sit at the table, and the eight-year-old would be the teacher, using her little sister as her assistant. They taught me to read and write before I was five. By the time I was old enough for kindergarten, I was transferred to the first grade, because I knew too much.

Later, much later, I learned that what Wallace Stevens wrote, "not ideas about the thing but the thing itself," is truer than the words we use to identify "the thing itself." Even now, I wrestle with the "thing" and its "idea," because I don't think I would have "seen" the thing if it hadn't been for the idea.

TALKING PROBABLY STARTED by "talking to self," creating meaning with sound—suddenly. All evolution starts suddenly. That evolution, Chomsky speculates, started with a small mutation in one person, one unique plan, a single endeavor of the mind that moved early Homo sapiens to making more symbolic equivalences. That ability to think symbolically was probably transmitted to offspring, both inherited and simulated, until there was an externalization of symbolic communication—language. That communication was, and still is, a significant factor in evolution.

Language is indirect evidence of the ability of every human to use sounds and symbols—the alphabet—to think symbolically, and to identify words with meaning-bearing elements, such as cow or atomic theory or love. Our mental constructions define all objects, for we see the world in terms of our perception of the external world.

But they are all creations of the mind. Words like river, tree, ocean, and rock are all our definitions of external objects. None are true representations of the world. Symbols do not represent the truth. As Wallace Stevens wrote, "Not ideas about the thing but the thing itself" is true.

Our nature is such that we do not "see" the world directly; we interpret the world through our own coding—language. One of the abstractions we value as a species is the notion of continuity. We give beginnings and endings and fill in the space between with meaning about what the imagined perception of fragmentary experiences and sights mean.

Children have "psychic continuity," as defined by Chomsky—that is, they can make "sense" and adapt to "impossible" realities, like fairy tales, or any possibility of "reality." Adults, however, impose a rigid continuity, because that is the nature of our cognitive systems; our minds are already preprogrammed to do so.

OUR INSTINCTIVE DRIVE for causal relationships and their beginnings is evident in every tribe, culture, and civilization throughout human history, while the history of human evolution shows that every grouping of humans attributes creation to some agent, some active intelligence that appears in religion. Religion is a cultural universal—belief beyond conscious belief, a spirit world we cannot grasp—that gives meaning to life. The "dust to dust" interpretation of experience is also a belief that ties humans together in the ultimate ending of all life; thus, belief in continuity has significant consequences in both the life that is being lived and the loss of it. Without it, there is no hope for the purpose and the objectives of human life itself. For a thinking species, outcomes are critical.

LANGUAGE, THEN, IS A PROCEDURE in our heads that contains both sound and image. The procedure is, as Chomsky calls it, digital infinity: Language generates more language, linguistic infinity. A burst of creativity occurred 75,000 years ago and initiated tool-making, symbolic representation (cave paintings), families, and language, thanks to the eruption of this new species of animal, one that could master thinking in symbols and then talking in symbols.

WHAT PURPOSE DOES LANGUAGE of the kind humans have constructed serve? No other known animal in the universe has the sophistication to identify "things" and the "unseen" hypothetical and theological manifestations of other worlds not made of things. Why do we have that ability? The existence of a creature with that kind of "instinct" for language raises theological speculations regarding the reasons intended.

The order and arrangement of all "things" on this earth have a purpose in relation to all other living and inert forms, and all forms have mathematically constructed systems that have the same properties. None, however, have the ability to speak of the unmanifest, of the scriptural (written by a Creator), of the objective of that Mystery to create a creature whose very nature is mysterious and whose purpose is undefined from the beginning of its creation.

Yet the language of that very creature itself speaks of a purpose. To investigate the unmanifest, the mysterious, the creation that is in perpetual creation, unending . . . to reach beyond boundaries and limitations to the boundless, limitless, infinite within, without . . . and to find itself within its Source . . .

SO WHAT IS THE PROBLEM with language, and what is "real"? We believe the "illusions" of symbols to be true. We can't help "seeing" this way. Our brains are endowed with fixed organic capacities, and the illusions of the world we see are believed by the culture, the species. Even when we don't believe that what we say we see could be real or plausible, we still "see" it that way. Remember when the world was flat, and everyone believed we could fall off? Even now, the dominant role of science is to discover the intelligible—as in, the world is a machine, and all we have to do is put the parts together to know its purpose. The world is not a machine. It has inherent mysteries that we can never plumb, but it's those mysteries that keep triggering us to question—to puzzle over possibilities.

OUR INHERENT SENSE OF INCOMPLETENESS, of strangeness, and the symbolic representations of our mind trigger what we don't know and must question; that is our nature and our only hope— the unknowable, the impalpable: the fundamental essences of an inherited mystery that is our Being—our Becoming . . . Our choice? To return to childhood wonder and delight, as we examine what we don't know, entering Earth's domain and becoming her child.

AND SO, MY DEAR WATKINS, our part? To see the myth in the mess and restore consciousness of the day in its innumerable disorder—an altar at the three crossroads, so we may keep looking and listening in many ways at once. This world is home to dreams, a world of ghosts, spirits, ancestors, demons, invisible by nature, open to possibility, nothing firm to hold on to, a mystery, unless we develop intuitive instruments for seizing the impalpable that slips through our fingers or burns at the touch, deeper than blood urges—a dream requiring no hope, no despair, beyond expectations—Only What Is—Things as Ideas.

PERHAPS NOW, I'm at the little table in that hallway. But this time, I am getting ready for kindergarten.

Scott Pedersen

THAT SOUND

I'M NO MEMORY SAVANT, just a guy who remembers every single second of a certain day in the summer of 1964. There must be a reason for that, right? Well, here is that day as I recall it.

I was at Buck's house. I had no brothers, so naturally I learned how to be a properly rambunctious boy from my cousin. He was twice my age and nearly twice my height. The outcome was a given when, on that particular day, we wrestled a bamboo fishing pole out of a jumbled corner of the garage. He snatched it and ran into the front yard. "Watch this!" he yelled, launching the pole from his palm.

I craned my neck to keep the pole in sight. Seconds later, it stabbed the ground in front of me. I reflexively jumped back, my shoulders snapping upward.

"Almost got ya," he said, laughing. "You oughta be more careful."

Before I could point out the ironic stupidity of this, Buck's father, Mort, appeared and ordered us into the family car.

Buck shrugged. "I guess we're leaving."

I'd started toward the car, when Buck snagged me by my sleeve.

"Don't say anything about the fishing pole. My dad doesn't like anybody messing with his gear, and I'll be the one in trouble, not you."

"Why?"

"Just get into the car. We're going to Shorty's." Shorty had a house nearby, next to Shorty's Salvage.

He gave us a friendly wave and led us into the living room. There, Buck and I fidgeted, while the men reminisced.

Soon, Buck tapped my shoulder and motioned toward the back door. We slipped out, raced past some hollyhocks and clothes lines, and entered the salvage yard through loose fence boards. There, we saw a delightful world filled with rusted cars, piles of tools, broken toys, small animal traps—you name it. We picked through piles of sundry items and clambered over unfamiliar machinery to find what was on the other side.

A Mount Rushmore cigarette lighter on the ground caught my eye. I scooped it up and stared at the faces of the presidents, scuffed but recognizable.

"There you are dreamin' again," said Buck. "What is that?"

I showed him the lighter.

"You should keep that," he said.

"Take it?"

"Sure, it's just a piece of junk. I mean, you like it, so it's cool."

"But that's stealing."

"Aw, a kid like you could rob a bank and not get into trouble."

I wasn't convinced but stuffed the lighter into my pants pocket, anyway.

Buck eyed some windows leaning against a wall. Their paint was flaking. A few muntins were cracked, but the panes were all intact. "Come with me," he called, and I ran after him.

He searched for a rock, picked up a hefty one, and let it fly. The glass exploded from its frame.

My eyes bulged. "Is it okay to break them?"

"Sure, they're just junk. They're gonna be thrown out anyway."

It seemed wrong, but this was my older cousin, a boy of great confidence, breaking windows. I picked up a rock and smashed a window. Soon, every pane was shattered.

Nothing could top that, so we went back inside the house.

We relaxed in the family room with our feet up, until we heard a muffled conversation coming from the front of the house.

"Is your dad still here?" I asked.

Buck whispered, "If he comes in here, don't say anything about the windows."

There was the slam of a door and then an angry voice. "Where are they?"

Mort tromped into the room and glared. He grabbed Buck by the arm and led him up the stairs to the second floor. I could hear yelling.

Shorty, drinking a beer in the dining room, raised his bottle and nodded to me.

I wandered over, thinking he was offering me something to drink. He laughed. "You're too young, little man."

Shorty leaned forward. "Your uncle's awfully mad about those old windows. I'm not, though. If I was you boys' age, I'd be doin' the same things." He took a long drink. "I was your age once, you know."

I looked around at the photos on the walls, pictures of the salvage yard, when it was owned by Shorty's father. I saw people standing around a Christmas tree, a man in a wooden fishing boat showing off the day's catch, and an outdoor sign that said, "Auto Salvage and Repairs." I looked back at Shorty, who smiled.

I reached into my pocket and pulled out the cigarette lighter. "Here," I said, holding it out to him.

He took it and said, "Thank you."

Gazing at Shorty, I tried to imagine being an adult. I knew it would happen but couldn't grasp what it would feel like or sense how long it would take. I believed I would be much taller and have a job. I would say all those adult-sounding things I heard every day from my parents. I would have children of my own. And, if it came to it, I might need to yell at a misbehaving boy.

I returned to the foot of the stairs, where I sat cross-legged on the floor. I noticed the grass stains on the knees of my jeans. That morning, I'd been on my knees in my own yard, feeling the sun on my back. A light wind lifted my shirt. I gazed down upon the grass, as if through the eyes of a giant. The grass became a forest, and the ants I saw through openings in its canopy were large beasts doing important things, as they rushed around. Maybe, they had their own salvage yard too, because their stuff must get old and wear out.

I heard a faint sound rising above distant trees—the soft, low-pitched drone of a small plane, very far off but coming closer. I looked up from the grass. How I loved that sound. It was the sound I'd heard the day before, when I'd sat scanning the sky, looking for its source. I believed the sound would be back the next day, along with the grass and the sky and the distant trees, and the day after that, and every day, for these are things that must never end.

Stomping footsteps broke the silence. Buck, red-faced with tears slipping down his cheeks, darted from the stairs. Then, Mort brushed by.

I thought for a moment. No punishment? Even for breaking windows? I enjoyed the feeling of privilege, of being the young one. To me there was every reason to believe I would stay young forever, or so far into the future that anything else was unimaginable.

The memory of that day is cemented in my mind. My feelings, as well as the details of the events, are still clear to me as I approach my sixtieth birthday. I can imagine the warmth of the sun on my back, while I peer at racing ants and, most vividly because of its suddenness, Buck hightailing it to avoid a plunging fishing pole. Over the years, I'd seen him develop into an even more adept dodger, and now I envied him for it.

One summer day, Buck came to see me, bringing news of a baby granddaughter. It was hard to look at the photos. My own daughter had recently given birth, but I had little hope of seeing the baby anytime soon.

"She looks like you," I said.

Buck's eyes brightened. "Remember when I used to play drums? Well, my buddies and I have a band, and we're not embarrassing at all. You gotta come hear us." His face darkened. "I mean, when you can."

"I will. You can count on it."

"Man, I used to make quite a racket. It drove my old man crazy. I don't know how I got away with it." He leaned forward in his chair. "I was a bad influence on you back then, wasn't I?"

"You shouldn't feel guilty about it. We were both just kids."

"Yeah, you're right. Just kids."

Buck glanced up at a wall clock. "No! Three o'clock already?"

A moment later, a prison guard was standing over us. "Okay, gentlemen, let's wrap it up."

As he left, Buck waved and called out, "Keep your chin up, Dillinger."

Back in my cell, I lay on my bunk and stared at the wall, my eyes settling on a calendar I'd hung by stuffing its top edge into a crack in the concrete. Next to it sat a roach, a sedentary creature, in no way industrious. I was pretty sure it was the same one I'd seen before in the same spot. I pounded the wall next to me to see if the roach would move. Nothing.

I pressed my eyes shut, when I heard the faint sound. It was the soft, low-pitched drone of a small plane, very far off but coming closer. The sound came in through the broken glass of a window near my cell. It was the same sound I'd heard the day before and, I was sure, would hear the next day. I believed the sound would be back every day, a sonic tally mark counting down the days left in my sentence until the last day, one so far into the future that it still seems unimaginable.

How I hate that sound.

Christina Petrides

MAKING DO

"There's no money in poetry," I am repeatedly told.
This is God's honest truth.
Even the most laurelled versifiers
barely scrape by on visiting academic salaries,
or must needs ply secular trades in long, dull, daylight hours.

But at night, they drum and mutter
incantations to themselves over cluttered, lamplit desks,
while nearby spouses snore under blankets, books, and cats,
periodically waking to mumble, "Honey, what are you doing?
It's late."

Fabrice Possain
THOUGHT

Joe De Quattro

GIFT OF YOUTH

SINCE HIS MOTHER'S DEATH earlier that spring, and now as an arid July gave way to a tropic-like August, Sal had been experiencing— at the age of forty and for the first time in his adult life really—just how silent and at times tedious the father-son dynamic could be. He wanted to believe, and in fact did believe, that love—love in this case a primordial thing—hung in the doorway of any room inhabited by such creatures, even those at war. At this particular point in time, it wouldn't have been entirely accurate to have qualified Sal and his father as "at war," but their overall absence of comfort certainly suggested people on the outs with one another. The culprit, and Sal often silently needed to find one, was really nothing more than that huge deficit of memories they'd failed to create, as each man in turn had for long stretches of time committed the sin of neglect, his father for the first twenty years of Sal's life, Sal for the last twenty. Initially, shortly after their estrangement had come to a forced end on the heels of the funeral, they had attempted several outings together, real father-son affairs, which to an outside observer might have come across as staged pseudo-comic exercises of failed men: A round of golf, while revealing a shared lack of patience and skill, ended with his father, who was eighty-five, badly straining his back; an afternoon at Fenway Park resulted in near sunstroke; and deep sea fishing's only real memory was the unmistakable cacophony of a hurled breakfast, as each man, unable to find even passable sea legs, sent his respective omelette, one eastern, one western, into an unexpectedly choppy Atlantic.

So it was with increasing dread that Sal had ventured from Boston to his father's apartment in Methuen, two nights a week. Here, they would sit out on the little stone balcony, facing one another in padded, metal folding chairs, the ticking, creaking silence climbing toward what appeared to be illimitable space. As Sal nursed a bad vodka tonic or screwdriver mixed out of generic brand liquor (the only other choice being beer to which he was allergic), a wake of odors from another era, talc, Barbisol, Polident, some out of fashion cologne, would waft through the open sliding doors to reach his nose. Sometimes, he would attempt to feed the silence with a fluff story—political scandal, unproven health fads, reality TV stars—none of which interested his father beyond a nod, or a single comment.

"She that one with the large rear end?" he'd say.

Sal, who taught Intro to Philosophy as an adjunct at a nearby college, had no classes to teach during the summer, so any chance for student anecdotes were tabled until the fall semester resumed (all the same his father had informed him that he had no interest in the subject), and neither of them seemed much inclined to discuss Sal's mother, the only real organic conversation piece between them. The one time, the only time, Sal had mentioned Marcia Cupp, his father's second wife, the old man flinched as if coming awake from an unsettling dream.

"Met a dry cleaner," he'd said. "Gone to Florida."

It was in moments such as these, as ice clinked in his glass like a buoy trying to alert someone to their presence, that given his father's age, Sal felt not so much like a son but as if he had a role, a job, and then one he wasn't sure he understood, was ready for, or wanted.

Perhaps it was simply to be there in the flesh, in constant view, an earlier representation with younger heart, clearer skin, brighter eyes, to be gazed upon by his father for as long as the man wished or time would allow.

Whatever the case, Sal's frustrations mounted. Despite this, or perhaps because of it, he felt often on the verge of opening the vault of juicy material in his possession, the one marked "Priscilla." He'd been tempted to do so countless times in the past but, immaturely engineered or legitimately organic, toward his father he felt none of that instinctual, disinterested, powerful trust which might have allowed confidences to flow freely. Besides, he knew that Priscilla, whose best and worst quality might have been her repressive nature, would have been utterly devastated if she knew he'd spoken about their private life.

BUT THIS ALL CHANGED, and rather quickly and ironically too, on the thick, warm August night when Sal learned an odd truth about his name. Certainly, it was the most intriguing thing his father had offered up all summer.

"Two names," Sal said incredulously. "For how long?"

"I figured your mother told you this years ago," his father said, an undeniable twinkle, however dark, setting up in his eye.

"How long?" Sal said again, as if the answer would completely impact his past and his future.

"If memory serves me," his father said, "until you were about four or so. Give or take a year."

"What? Are you kidding me? Is this a joke?"

"Calm down," his father said. "Just inside the house. Never in public."

"Still," Sal said, "isn't that abuse or something?"

"Abuse?" his father said, as if he'd never heard the word before. "Clearly, you were too young to remember, so how could it be abuse? Besides, what do you want from me? Your mother could be tough."

Sal sat back. "Two names. Jesus."

His father nodded conspiratorially. "No idea what she liked so much about Salvatore. I do know she hated Vladimir—which is what I wanted—because it was the name of an army buddy of mine she absolutely despised. We fought a lot about that, I tell you. You know, your mother wasn't the saint everybody always thought she was."

Sal ignored this, and though he didn't like thinking of his father as victorious, he said, "So how did Sal stick?"

"It was the name you responded to most. That's all. It wasn't no trick."

Quiet descended then, for a few long minutes, though Sal, even despite this odd information, couldn't help noting that it wasn't so awkward and uncomfortable.

"For what it's worth," his father said softly, contritely, "being able to tell you this means a lot to me."

Sal didn't press. He felt torn, not sure if he should appreciate what his father had just told him or feel betrayed. Nevertheless, he couldn't deny—even as he tried to do so—a massive filial symbiosis welling within, maybe for the first time, allowing for a wall to drop (confession, that's what the soul wanted), all at once making him feel less the guarded adult and more a freely trusting child willing to double down.

"Priscilla's convinced I'm cheating on her," he forced out quickly, as if afraid he'd change his mind.

"You are?"

"No," Sal said annoyed. "I said she thinks I am. Are you not hearing well tonight?"

"So you're not?"

"No." It was the truth. He hadn't ever once strayed, but he and Priscilla were living now, living consistently, as if he had. What made it all the more frustrating was that he had no idea what the root cause of her growing paranoia and insecurity might be. Recently, there had been an, at first, impossible to explain text message on his phone—"Hey, are we still on?"—to which Sal had replied, "I'll be there." Under heavy questioning ("hey" was a feminine greeting, Priscilla told him), during which his stammering and faulty memory served as death sentence, he eventually remembered (though it seemed like fabrication) that the message was from a male student he'd helped with a paper on William Hazlitt. Shortly after this, there was an awkward encounter outside a department store on Boylston Street one Saturday afternoon, when Priscilla came upon Sal, who'd waited out front, talking with an attractive female, one of his students, just then passing by. Altogether innocent. Nothing shady or unhanded. But at the sight of Priscilla, at realizing who she was, the young woman blushed horribly, horrifically behind horn-rimmed glasses, surprising even Sal, who'd begun to introduce her, before scurrying off.

"The texter, I presume," Priscilla had said with satisfaction.

These little incidents, though, could hardly be inspiration for such dark and comprehensive marital suspicion and doubt. The insecurity, the paranoia, they were simply there one day (even before the text message, the scene outside the store) like hidden parts of Priscilla's personality she could no longer contain. Lately, there were nights when, in more sea-thrown moments, she would bring her face close to Sal's eyes and sniff deeply. Priscilla, she begrudgingly explained after the first of these inspections, had come to believe that the eyes were receptacles of impossible to wash off sex odors, as if even after a hot shower the eyes acted as a kind of olfactory black box, intrepidly recording evidence of one's sexual escapades (real or imagined), where the scent of feet, cupped breasts, clutched backs of knees and thighs could be found. And when she failed to unearth any sort of damning evidence against him, she only became critical, as if wanting to hurl Sal into the arms of a phantom lover: "You're losing your hair; you're getting a belly."

And so they co-existed now with rage, frigidity, hostility, silence. A sitcom could set her off. An episode of CSI. A news story. Eventually, Sal found himself at odds with his innocence.

"No," he said again, looking out from his father's little balcony toward the sky. The warm August day had left it smudged here and there with gaseous purple and peach. "I haven't done anything." He paused. "Not like I haven't thought about it, though."

Now his father made a noise, a loud expulsion of air through puckered lips. "You say that like you're the only man who's ever thought about straying. After a certain point, who hasn't?"

"I know, but—"

"What," his father said. "Are you so naïve?"

"No," Sal said, showing a bit of anger now. "I don't mean it the way you're thinking. Everyone's human. I get it. But in this case, the way she's been acting, it's like I have done something. Cheated."

His father was quiet a moment as he thought this over. "So she's upset, even though there's no proof? That what you're saying?"

"Very upset," Sal said. "A lot of the time now. Almost always, it seems." He took a silent breath. "And honestly?"

"Yes?" His father was deeply interested now.

"It only makes me want to. That's what I meant when I said that it's not like I haven't thought about it. I never used to think about it, but if I have to be punished for something I haven't done, shouldn't I at least get something in return?" Sal paused, visibly upset at having said this. It was flawed logic, and he knew it. "I don't mean that. I love her. Just—I'm not sure what to do anymore. All I do is deny, which is the truth, but then something lingers. What's crazy is that it's like she's made her way into my fantasies, these boring middle-aged fantasies I have, every man has, and when that happens I don't know what a person's supposed to do. I need to have my own mind, don't I? Privately? It's exhausting. Is it right for her to be going in there, into my mind, and rearranging my private thoughts? Making me feel guilty just for thinking?"

Sal had spoken loudly and more voluminously than he had (collectively perhaps) in all the times he'd been with his father over the last weeks and months. He grew quiet now, having said what had been pressing on him so long, anticipating a fatherly or somewhat fatherly battery of questions aimed at Priscilla's past, before she'd met Sal, when she might have incurred a penetrating wound.

"I went through something similar with your mother," his father said.

Sal sat up, readying himself for some sort of confession.

"It's hereditary."

"Hereditary," Sal said. "What is?"

"Thing that's causing your problem." From a little bowl on a table he kept beside his chair, his father took up a handful of nuts—almonds and filberts—and rifled these into his mouth. "Gift of youth." The full mouth at once made these words difficult to decipher, but it also lent them a certain credibility and weight.

"Gift of what?"

"Youth," his father said. He dusted his hands. "Maybe curse of youth is better." He paused in thought. "Yeah, curse. But it's definitely a gift, too."

"Sorry, I'm not following."

"Look at me. Never think I was eighty-five, would you?"

Sal looked him over. "I couldn't really say."

"Of course, I don't look it," his father said. "And you, you're forty, but you still look like a kid."

"To you, maybe."

"I bet to a lot of people. I see guys your age who actually look fifty-five, and I know seventy year olds who look older than me."

"Fine, so what?"

"So," his father said, "either way, it's the thing that makes us both attractive to women and, in the case of your wife and mine, your mother, extremely repulsive."

Sal had little or no idea what to do with this piece of information, how any of it applied to the intimate things he'd just revealed about his marriage. He felt embarrassed.

"Take your grandfather, for instance, my father."

"What about him? Didn't Grandpa die when he was forty-five?"

"Sure," his father said, "but what youthfulness until then. Thing I'm talking about keeps you young when all the other guys go on aging. Gift of youth."

"If you just mean sex—"

"I don't mean sex," his father said.

Sal put nothing, or very little at least, into what his father was saying here, but he couldn't help being impressed by his conviction.

"You have strong ideas about things." It was something he would always be glad he'd said, for he meant this in the most positive way.

"Most women find us irresistible," his father went on eagerly. "Am I right?"

"I'm afraid that hasn't been my overall experience."

"Sure," his father said. "They do. Most women, that is, but the ones we're married to. Your girl, your mother. They don't know how to handle it. The thing don't fade over time, either. In fact, seems to get stronger. Just look at me. So, they get moody. Start blaming us for stuff."

"It's more than moodiness," Sal said, trying to redirect the conversation, however gently. "It's just how Priscilla is now. Who she is. It makes me depressed."

"You really never stepped out on her?"

"No, I said. And I won't. But it's gotten so bad—her paranoia, my desires—that for the last year or so, every time I find myself just staring after an attractive woman, I end up buying Priscilla a book."

"A book?"

"I can't even say why a book, specifically. Maybe less obvious than flowers or something. I don't know. Maybe nostalgia for how it used to be with us."

His father offered a curious look.

"We used to read together a lot," Sal said in explanation. "Books as an innocent qualifier or something. Priscilla likes espionage."

"Espionage," his father said, both with deep understanding and naïve curiosity.

"Yeah," Sal said, "Le Carre, some Fleming. Detective novels, too. Our shelves are full of Hammett and Chandler. James M. Cain."

None of these names appeared to register, but it didn't matter. "I think I've bought her twenty novels in the last six months alone, to give you an idea what my mind's been doing. Sounds crazy, but it helps. Or, helped, I should say. Lately, the books just sit there, representing what I'm imagining myself doing behind her back."

"You want to leave her?"

"No," Sal said, passionate but steadfast. "Not at all. But I don't know how to get past this."

His father pushed out his bottom lip. It looked dry. "Maybe I can help."

Sal slit his eyes at him. "That's why I'm telling you, Dad. Talking can sometimes—"

"No," his father said quietly. "I mean help literally. Hands on. See what I can do. I haven't seen her since the funeral, and you do realize you've never had me over. Two birds, as they say."

The question of apartment guests was moot. Marital discord aside, Sal and Priscilla had existed in their dusty, crumbly three hundred seventy five square foot apartment (previously four hundred, as if getting smaller) for four years without a single visitor. (They had fewer and fewer friends, and Priscilla always traveled to visit her family in the Midwest.) This absence of guests stemmed solely from shame, from the fact that neither of them felt they could stomach the stark reality of seeing someone they knew walk among such ruins.

"Talk to her, that sort of thing," his father was saying. "See if you got a bigger problem than you think. Hands on. You are my boy, after all."

Sal was nodding driftily, no longer really present in the conversation. He was trying to prepare himself mentally for what sounded like an eventual and unavoidable visit, at which point his failure, his life failure (did he really care what his father thought?), would be on display in all its resplendent glory. At the same time, though, he never believed this would occur, never believed his father, or anyone for that matter, would set foot in his apartment.

"Let me think about it," Sal said, and with that, he let himself out into the tropical August night and drove home to Boston, speeding excessively on I-93, the windows down and the howling wind battering his head, a head that was full now of odd images and feelings.

Back at the apartment, he was surprised to find Priscilla, almost always asleep by ten these days, still awake.

"Phone woke me," she said and flipped off the bathroom light. "Your father."

Sal's heart began to thump in his throat, though he was unable to determine if it was pulmonary joy or anxiety. "Is he okay?"

She got back into bed. "Grand." Through the darkness, through her nose, she let out a heavy sigh, longer and louder it seemed than the one she'd emitted earlier that day or the night before. "He's coming for dinner next Saturday night."

THE FOLLOWING WEEK Sal opted to see his father only once. Right off, he noted that the intimacies forged during their last visit had been replaced once again by long uncomfortable silences, by commonplace observations, by the forced, the awkward. At one point toward the end of the night, trying without success to find the right emotion about his two name past and now feeling raw that his father had gone over his head to get himself invited to dinner (Priscilla may not have wanted that either but what, when put on the spot, could she have done about it?), Sal began to preemptively, gently, offer a warning. Just as he did so, however, his father, having displayed once or twice a surprising ability, given their previous distance, to diagnose and respond to his son's unspoken sentiments or concerns, said, "Don't worry, I won't say anything that'll embarrass you."

On Saturday, though, within minutes of arriving, he began to go back on his word. Sal had followed him down the long hallway into the apartment, searching for, as if it had somehow escaped him all this time, a buoyant feeling of pride. At the threshold of the small, cramped living room, his father stopped short.

"Boy, they really don't pay teachers much, do they?"

Immediately, he then became absorbed in the overflowing bookshelf, which practically swallowed the tiny living room. Sal noted that, when his father looked at inanimate objects, a golf club, a fishing pole, a dinner menu, now these books, the expression he wore was that of a person being looked at.

"Espionage," he said loudly.

"Espionage?" Priscilla said, entering the room. She smiled. "What espionage?"

But his father said nothing further, only turned to face her. For the occasion he had on all white: white Izod shirt open at the throat, white cotton Bermuda shorts, white socks, white tennis sneakers with thick soles.

The exposed arms and legs Sal noted with a bit more gravity now, perhaps because there was a third person present, were knobby, bony, curving in odd and in some spots painful looking directions.

The skin in places looked oniony, as if at the touch of a finger it would flake away. Still, with the tan from frequent afternoons out on his balcony, the overall effect was of a weathered handsomeness.

"Don't you look great, Bert," Priscilla said.

Sal hadn't heard anyone use his father's name in some time. It made him want to laugh out loud. Laugh at the strange sounding sound of Bert. Like a bodily expulsion. Bert!

"I hear your back's much better." She was reaching. By then, his father's back strain suffered during their golf outing was very old news that hadn't been replaced by anything of note. Things between Sal and Priscilla had been so fractured that Sal hadn't told her, for instance, what he'd discovered the previous week about once having two names. He didn't think it mattered. It seemed so much of what was communicated between them now went unheard.

"I heal up good," his father said, and did a little twist at the waist. "Always have. Your good thoughts helped."

At this, Priscilla glanced at Sal.

"You did send good thoughts," his father said, noticing the look, "didn't you, darling?"

"Of course," Priscilla said. "Of course I did, Bert."

"All you ever thought about," his father went on.

"All and only," Priscilla said, getting into it.

They laughed. Sal watched them. In the tiny space, three people felt nearly impossible, and Sal didn't quite know where to put himself. He sat on the couch. An old air conditioner labored in one of the windows. The room was warm.

Suddenly, his father, silently and with head back and arms outstretched, began to pirouette. The sight brought Sal to his feet.

"Dad?"

"Bert?"

His father turned two, three more times, then stopped.

"One of you I can see," he said, looking directly at Priscilla. "But two of you in this place? I don't know how you've done it for three years, my dear."

"Four," Priscilla said.

"How does she do it?" his father said turning to Sal.

"Why don't you sit down, Dad," Sal said, clearly annoyed.

His father turned back to Priscilla.

"You must bump into one another constantly," he said. "So small."

"We've learned to keep our distance," Priscilla said, without looking in Sal's direction. "Anyway, I hope you like salmon, Bert."

"Oh, I love fish. All kinds."

She turned back to the kitchen.

"What do you think you're doing," Sal said, grasping his father's wrist.

"What?"

"I asked you not to embarrass me."

"Have I?"

The sincerity of this was unnerving. "Yes," Sal said, "you have. "Espionage? The crack about my income? Your little Bolshoi Ballet here. Do you not know what you're saying or doing?"

"Well, so what," his father said. "They don't pay teachers enough. Isn't that true?"

"That's not the point."

Priscilla came in with a glass of Chardonnay for his father.

"Oh," he said, taking the glass. "Would you have any beer, my love?"

But Sal answered. "No beer, Dad. I'm allergic, remember?"

"Oh right, I forgot," his father said, without taking his eyes off Priscilla. "But I'm not." He looked at Sal. "And I am your guest. Such a warm night. Bottle of beer would be perfect."

"This is white wine," Sal said. "Chilled. See, look at the glass. Condensation."

Ignoring him, his father turned back to Priscilla. "You look like you could use a cold beer yourself. Wouldn't you agree it would hit the spot, my sweet?"

"I told him to get beer," she said. "You're a beer drinker. Even I know that, Bert." She looked at Sal. "How 'bout it?"

"What?"

"Beer run." She took back the glass of Chardonnay. "I'll have this while I finish cooking."

The two men watched her, as she went back to the kitchen.

"Do you really want it," Sal said.

"What? Beer?"

"Yes, beer."

"In all the meals you and I have had together, when have you seen me drink wine? I'm parched. Don't that AC go any higher?"

Sal ignored this. "I'll get your beer," he said, "but no more antics. Don't say or do anything else, understand?"

"But now, I'll have a chance to talk to her. Find out what's going on between the two of you. Alone, I mean."

"You heard me. Not a word."

"But you said you wanted my help."

"No," Sal said, "I didn't. And that was very private stuff I told you. Priscilla would go through the roof, if she knew I told you any of that."

"Fine. But I want to help, and that's what I'm going to do."

"I don't need your help here, Dad. Okay?"

"You don't, maybe. But what about her? She might be begging for it, and frankly it don't sound like you'd have any idea. Let me give it a shot."

Sal rose to his feet. "Stop," he said. "I'm angry you're here at all."

"Angry? What, you ashamed of me or something?"

"You know what I'm talking about. I'm angry that you went over my head and got yourself invited, when it should have come from me. Don't play games."

"Okay, okay," his father said, but then stood up quickly and broke for the kitchen. Sal, firmly but gently grabbed hold of his left bicep. It felt like a deflated bicycle tire still on the rim.

"Where you going?"

"To talk to her," his father said. "I told you. It's what I planned."

"What? Are you not hearing well? I want you to stay here, right here, until I get back."

"All right." His father thought a moment. "But I'm going to talk to her, whether you're here or not." He smiled. "It'll be fine."

"It won't be fine. Sit down."

His father lowered himself to the edge of the couch, but just as Sal turned toward the hallway, he was up again, moving sneakily for the kitchen. Sal, seeing this, gave no protest. He only waited a few moments before quietly crossing back to just inside the doorway of the bedroom. Given his father's stealthy approach, he half expected to hear Priscilla—absorbed in running water, the clattering of pans and dishes, the accordion squeak of the oven door—scream, but as she turned and came into view, she only smiled, while the old man stood leaning against the kitchen table and watched her.

"Bert," she said, "you startled me. Has he gone for the beer?"

"He's gone, my lovely."

Unlike the look his father possessed when staring at inanimate objects, the expression on his face now in the tiny kitchen, an expression that seemed to ooze throughout his entire being, was that of an enchanted boy. Surprisingly lustful, but innocent too.

Sal, unseen, remained where he was in the bedroom doorway. He watched, transfixed, mesmerized. After a few moments, he inched forward a bit. From here, he wasn't able to see Priscilla, who had turned back to the sink. Only his father, the broad forehead beginning to glaze, to glow with sweat from the oven and the heat of the evening. He was speaking in a low voice, lower than usual, but captivating enough given Priscilla's responses, which were more audible and clear: "Oh, no, not too hard. But I'm not a very good cook. We hardly use the kitchen, actually. Of course it's for you, Bert, who else?"

And the look on his father's face, man or boy it didn't matter. Wanting.

Sal was unsure, exactly, what he was seeing, what this look was. He felt momentarily stuck, physically unable to leave for this simple errand, so fearful that his father would unload everything he had told him about the book buying, about his desire to act on his fantasies.

"What kind of beer," he finally said, loudly. His voice was hollow, almost cracking. He half expected his father to flinch, but he only remained where was, in profile, leaning against the kitchen table and staring at the backside of Priscilla, who was momentarily out of view.

"Any kind," his father said evenly. "Cold."

Priscilla reappeared then, to the left of his father. She placed a bowl of steamed Brussels sprouts on the table. As if seeing her for the first time that evening, Sal noted that she had on a terribly short blue terry cloth dress. The skin of her shoulders, which were bare, shone brightly over the bone from the sun and from scrubbing with a loofah. She was shoeless. Her toenails were pale pink.

Something filled Sal, then. A desire to scream perhaps. Something awful, anyway. He watched his father watching the smiling Priscilla, who was for the next few moments back and forth, in and out of view, as she finalized the spread on the table. She was smiling and licking her fingers without self-consciousness, though clearly aware that his father watched her with deep interest.

Unsettled, unable to look anymore, Sal went down to the street for the beer. Trust was an uneasy commodity between fathers and sons, he thought. Perhaps moreso than between any other parent-child combination. It required something. Time. Without it, two men, even those as blood-bonded as father and son, could easily become enemies. What was the old man doing?

"Hello Sally," Rose said. Rose worked evenings at the small liquor store a block away, and was in the process, a long one due to a lack of finances, as he'd inform anyone who might listen, of changing over from male to female. The metamorphosis had been arduous, Rose told him, but not without evidence. Not without spectacular display. Sal didn't know at that point what phase Rose was in now, but he could say with certainty that some time ago, he'd been Ron, a man, and then, the next month, Rose, a man on the verge of womanhood. There, Rose remained suspended, indefinitely it seemed.

"I'm getting my teeth done," Rose told him and grinned a toothless mouth, the earnestness of which precluded revulsion. "Next week."

"Good," Sal said, not knowing if teeth had anything large or important to do with the process. He put money on the counter next to a six pack of Miller Lite, the only beer he ever saw his father drink.

"You look glum," Rose said. "Bag?"

"No bag," Sal said. "Really? Glum?"

"Maybe it's me," Rose said, as he nevertheless cumbersomely put the six pack into a bag.

"No," Sal said, "you might be right."

"Serious?"

"I'm not sure. Going on a while now."

Glum as he might have been, something remarkable suddenly occurred to Sal. He'd not seen Rose in several weeks, not since his father had revealed the truth about his name. As a result, he had no choice but to feel differently in his own skin. Altered. Even if he was too young to remember being called by two names, something deeply innocent had been exploded right before his eyes. That part, that self, was lost now. This, however, wasn't what struck him as he stood there in the store. What struck him, and while certainly it was gravely different, was that he and Rose had something profound in common now. Before this point, that was something Sal could never have imagined. Now, he felt a poignant connectedness, not just to Rose, but to something unquantifiably deep within himself. It seemed to spill into him, fall over him, like the first glimpse of daylight in winter.

"Tell me something, Rose," Sal said. "Which do you prefer? Which name? Salvatore or Vladimir?"

Rose thought this over with quick but sincere interest. "I mean, they're both nice. I knew a Sal when I was a kid, though I never called him Salvatore, and the only Vladimirs I've heard of are the famous ones. I'd say Sal. Yeah, definitely Sal." Rose paused. "Know what name I really like, though? Falcon."

"Falcon?"

"Like the bird," Rose said. "Or Stuyvesant. Cool name."

Sal nodded. "How about from now on you call me Falcon?"

"But I love Sal," Rose said, as if the suggestion of Falcon somehow had legal permanence.

"As a nickname or something," Sal said. "Between us."

"Okay," Rose said, "I like that. Well, goodbye, Falcon."

"Goodbye, Rose."

BACK UPSTAIRS, SAL WAS ENTIRELY UNPREPARED for what he found. Or, rather, for what he didn't. In such a small apartment, it was easy to detect changes, acoustical or otherwise, almost immediately. While the living room was empty, the door to his and Priscilla's bedroom, which they always kept open in order to create an illusion of space, was closed now, shut up tight. After a try of the knob, he found it was locked. Nervous, Sal rapped hard before hearing a quick sound off to his left from the kitchen. Silverware, a tablespoon no doubt, moved across the countertop. Something like that. He stepped inside where the entire meal—the salmon, the mashed potatoes, the Brussels sprouts, the wine—had been laid out on the table in a state just prior to consumption. Steam rose from the plates. And here, leaning against the sink, he found his father, who, when he saw Sal raised his hands, palms out, as if to prevent himself from being struck.

"More a curse, I guess," he said in an odd voice. "I didn't say anything, I swear. I just—"

"What?" Sal said. His voice was calm, concerned, though he felt something horrible drain from his chest to his stomach. "Dad? What's happened?"

"Sal," Priscilla called. He noted, despite the peculiar scene, that there was little or no distress in her voice.

Sal looked a moment more at his father. "What did you say?"

"Nothing," his father said. "I swear. I didn't say anything, but maybe it really is a curse. I'm sorry."

Sal left him then, unsure what his father meant, and went to the bedroom. Priscilla sat on the edge of the bed. The room was dark.

"He got a little overly friendly," she said calmly, "but it's fine. Don't freak out."

His focus still on what his father might have said to Priscilla, Sal at first took this information innocently. "What do you mean, friendly? Like eighty-five-year-old man friendly? Like that? He's always making little jokes with women—"

"Not old man friendly," Priscilla said. "More serious."

"Wait. He hit on you? Legitimately? Is that what you're saying?"

"It was ugly for a minute," Priscilla said, "but I think that had more to do with the surprise of it. I swear I was so shocked that I sort of forgot where I was. Calm down, Sal. It was nothing I couldn't handle, believe me. Creeped me out more than anything."

"Yeah, right," Sal said and went for the door. "It must have been way worse than that if you had to lock yourself in here."

"Stop," she said. "What else could I have done? It only lasted a few seconds. Don't be stupid, and don't embarrass him."

"Embarrass him?"

"He's a sweet old man."

"Sweet?"

"He's old," Priscilla said. "And he's your father."

"What did he say, 'Cill?" Sal, deep in the moment, was nevertheless aware of using this long neglected nickname.

"Say?" She was looking at him curiously.

"I mean do," he said. "Tell me." Here Sal recalled the way his father had said so matter-of-factly that he was going to talk to Priscilla, whether he was there or not. The calculated quality of this only made whatever was being revealed now that much more upsetting.

"Use your imagination," Priscilla said. "It doesn't matter what he did."

"But you're saying he put his hands on you," Sal said. "Where? Up your dress? Down the front? Show me."

"Stop it," Priscilla said. "If I could handle it, does it matter? Don't make a scene. Please. Just, maybe, dinner's not such a good idea now. Could you tell him without embarrassing him too much?"

"You want me to take him home?"

"I think it would be best."

Sal was quiet a moment. "Tell me what he did."

"It's the kind of thing, believe me, that if we make an issue of it now, in the morning we're going to feel like idiots. Not to mention terrible. Like we made something out of nothing. Trust me. He's an old man. Let it be. Let him have this."

"Let him have it? Are you nuts? Let him have it? I'm going to—"

"You're going to do nothing," Priscilla said calmly, but angrily. "Drop it. Go, take him home. Tell him I'm not feeling well. And don't say anything in the car. Can you do that?"

Sal was quiet. Despite the few moments of irritation, he noted that there was a closeness, a warmth, to the way Priscilla was speaking to him. Any coldness, any distance, was absent. Crises.

Sal thought. Crises and confession. These are what the soul, the human heart, required.

IN THE CAR ON THE WAY BACK to his father's apartment (the old man took the news of dinner's postponement without protest), Sal was intentionally silent. For one thing, he was embarrassed, for his father, for his wife, for himself. Mainly, though, he didn't want to betray Priscilla and the way she wanted to handle things. But he was angry. En route to the highway, he drove dangerously fast beneath the night damp summer elms.

"Used to think it was a gift," his father was saying. "Maybe so, maybe so. At one time. At one time, women found it irresistible. They did. So it was a gift, I guess. Now, though, now maybe just a curse, like I was saying." He looked over at Sal who kept his eyes fixed on the road. "What can I say? I'm an old man. I get lonely. I don't have needs?"

Sal wasn't listening. He was trying to come up with a way to satisfy his anger, his contemptuous feelings. What could he do? Enter another phase where he acted like the old man didn't exist? Hadn't both men rather monstrously used up all the neglect one human being should be allowed to inflict upon another? No, that wouldn't do. It would break the man's heart, and besides, how much time did he have left? It very well could be his last or penultimate summer. Sal turned and looked at his father's profile, the big, bulbous nose, hawkish eyes that seemed no longer possessed of peripheral capability. The overhead streetlights, as they passed under them, reflected in the glassy, opaque lens of the left eye. The lips were still moving, forming words silently. Sal leaned over and tried to hear above the wind coming in through the open window. Something similar to what he'd been muttering up in the apartment? Maybe, and this, for a moment, brought Sal's anger back. He opened his own mouth, intending to begin telling his father in a loud, clear voice just how disgusted he was by what he had done. "How dare you," were the first words he got ready in his mind, but by the time he had the window up, he'd pushed these feelings down. His father glanced over at him. Sal looked away, gripped the wheel. No, even despite how dumbfounded and angry he felt, he didn't want to break what was left of the man's heart, and in this particular situation with Priscilla, he didn't want to embarrass him, either. So, he just kept quiet. Picked up speed. And eventually let him have it.

Richard Risemberg

THE SERVICE PORCH

EVERYONE SHOULD BE ALLOWED one blatant peculiarity. Mine was my lint-ridden refuge, the service porch. It was the one place I felt completely at ease, if only because it was the one place in the apartment where no one would want to barge in on me, or need to. I had put myself in charge of laundry, and the washer and dryer were there, as well as a utility sink and some old warped shelves that held bottles or cartons of soap, bleach, ammonia, floor wax, and other useful but ultimately boring substances, materials associated with harsh smells and crusty recesses. The service porch barely existed in the minds of the rest of the family, since no one but me ever used the back door, anyway. To them, it was a blank gray mystery, best ignored. And so, I placed a chair there, one that I had found in the alley behind our building. I cleaned it up, using the resources of my little hideaway.

The service porch was a space about eight by eight feet square, with two tired-looking sash windows on one wall, allowing a view of the building across the common walkway. There was a flimsy door that led to the back stairwell and the sturdier locking door that led to our kitchen. The service porch and the stairwell were both painted battleship gray, but the paint was old and cracked, flaking off in places to show dry rot underneath.

I had jammed a row of books between two bottles of cleaning product on the shelf. The chair and books were all I needed to be happy, besides a working light bulb, if I went out there after dark. Sometimes, I took a glass of wine and parked it on the clothes dryer, but that was an indulgence. It was generally enough to get away from the family for an hour or so, read a few poems or a short story, and listen to the sounds of the building around me. It was an old wooden apartment building, stucco on the outside but as resonant as a guitar, and I could hear dribs and drabs of everything that went on around me.

On any given afternoon, I could hear Roland in the upstairs back apartment, practicing his flute. During the evenings, the sounds of cooking or dishwashing came from all directions. Later on, the whining of televisions resonated, while in the mornings, I could hear Lila's blender going off in the apartment next to ours. Sometimes, I even sat there in the middle of the night, if I couldn't sleep, privy to an occasional snore or the grunts of love resounding through tired wood. The light bulb was old and feeble, just enough to read by, and that somehow made the place more cozy at night. I didn't always read, though; there were times when I just sat in my old chair, breathing and listening. With no traffic noise to overwhelm the small sounds of darkness, I could hear pipes running, toilets flushing, footsteps inside or outside, the creaks of the building itself, and the whoosh of the communal water heater turning on, usually just after dawn when my neighbors started taking their daily showers.

The water heater was in a cellar, just below my hideaway. I had gone down into the cellar once, just to see where the rest of the stairway led, and had seen it—a fat cylinder, ensconced in the corner of a rough concrete box, no bigger than my service porch. There was a light bulb, that apparently never turned off, screwed into a cheap ceiling fixture as a sort of votive candle above the thing. This water heater was a dull, forgotten appliance that we all depended on. These things interest me, a world we ignore that is wound invisibly into our daily lives.

My habits being what they were, it was no surprise that I should be the one to discover the secret lodger. I began to hear sounds that were not typical of our building, shuffling whispery rustles in the night, an occasional faint moan, the pad-pad sound of careful footsteps. Once in a while, the clunk of a riser I had noticed was loose enough to be a bit of a hazard. There was no lock on the cellar door down at the bottom of the stairs. There was nothing in there but the water heater and a moldy cardboard box holding burned-out light bulbs, and now, perhaps, a person.

This would not be surprising. Our neighborhood hosted a number of homeless folk, some of whom I had spoken to enough to know their names. There were two who talked to themselves all day, though they could break away from their invisible interlocutors and answer you cogently if you said, "Good morning." There was one younger fellow with a long, matted beard. He stared at the sidewalk all day while smoking cigarettes, and he never answered a greeting. A couple of them struck me as being drunks, though I never saw them drinking. At least half of them had just run out of money after losing a job or having had a run-in with medical billing. At least that's what they told me, and from what I read in the papers, it was common enough.

I decided to see which of them had settled in our basement, near the whoosh of the water heater and under the eternal bulb. It would be dirty and uncomfortable, but it would be better than the street, which was also dirty and uncomfortable.

I must admit to feeling a bit of apprehension, since it could be someone new and perhaps dangerous, but after the fourth time I heard the odd rustling sound, I made up my mind to play greeter and say *hello*. It was early in the evening, though already dark, when

I let myself out the back door of my service porch and made a point of clomping loudly down the cellar steps. I had taken my big flashlight. It was a police model that could double as a club. I didn't anticipate any trouble, but I followed the old Boy Scout dictum of "Be Prepared."

A flashlight looks innocent enough when one is going down into a badly-lighted cellar. It would allow me to be friendly. You can't be friendly while carrying a gun or a knife, not that I owned a gun or that kind of knife. So, I blundered on down, opened the door with no particular care, and stepped into the cramped and musty room. The light was out, so I switched on the flashlight, which was a very powerful one—I had justified the expense by stressing its utility in case of an earthquake, but really I just enjoyed the way it could light up a whole building from half a block away. It certainly lighted the cellar up. I heard a gasp from the corner opposite the door and saw the blue nylon of a sleeping bag, looking like a giant grub curled up in the corner. A mop of yellow hair showed in its mouth, not clean hair but well-brushed. A girl's voice said, "Leave me alone. I'm just trying to sleep!" A young girl's voice. More than a kid, maybe a teenager.

"And just who are you?" I asked. I succeeded in sounding polite and unperturbed. Of course, I had been rehearsing my lines in my head.

"Tell me who you are first."

"I'm your upstairs neighbor," I said. I was proud of having thought up that unrevealing but true response.

A narrow little face, more pretty than not but no beauty, shook itself free from the maw of the sleeping bag. She squinted against the light. "You're blinding me."

"The light bulb's out."

"I just unscrewed it a bit. So I could sleep. Screw it back in."

I did as I was told. The old bulb flickered on, and I doused the flashlight. The girl's eyes blinked a few times, and then her face settled itself. She was prettier when she didn't squint, though she was a little pop-eyed. "So, who are you?" I repeated.

She looked me right in the eye. "I guess I'm your downstairs neighbor, then." She crossed her arms inside the sleeping bag and leaned back against the crusty wall. She had a little knapsack next to her and a couple of glossy magazines on the floor.

"That a fact?" I said.

"Guess so." She lifted her chin in a gesture of defiance that was itself a bit scripted.

I pretended to ignore it. "How old are you? You look awfully young."

"None of your business." She shuffled herself up, so that she could sit straighter, but she stayed in the bag.

"Run away from home?"

A long sigh. "Yeah. Like everyone else, I guess."

I thought of the street kids I had seen in the nightclub district. "Not everybody runs away from home. I never did."

"You didn't grow up in my house. Bet you would've if you did."

"Everybody thinks their parents are oppressive at some point. And I guess they are."

"It was worse than that. But it was that too. Just don't ask. I'm not going back."

"The street is better?"

The chin went up again. "Yeah. At least I can walk away from trouble there."

"And hide in my basement?"

"You the building owner?" The chin dropped.

"No, I just live here. It was a figure of speech."

"You've got little kids. I hear them."

"Two. The younger one just started kindergarten."

"Let them enjoy their lives, while they can."

"I try," I said.

Her shoulders writhed out of the bag. She was wearing two old t-shirts, one over the other, both white and in need of washing. Her shoulders were bony. I asked, "You been eating enough?"

"Just junk food. I thought I liked it, 'til I got out and that was all I could buy. I had a bag of Cheetos for dinner tonight with a bottle of orange juice. They were stale. They're always stale at the kind of shops that let us in."

"And you've got the money to live on junk food?"

"I saved my allowance for eight months, so I could run away. My friends got mad at me, 'cause I wouldn't go out with them anymore."

"And when it runs out?"

The chin dropped a bit. "Then, I don't know. I'm being careful with it."

The phone chimed in my pocket. I pulled it out, an automatic text message reminding me to go to the dentist next week. I decided to be clever while I had the phone out and looked at the Bluetooth settings. There was a new device nearby, a phone called TinyTina. I stuck the thing back into my pocket. Before I could say anything, I heard footsteps in my apartment. We both looked up. I knew the layout of the place and could follow them from the main bedroom, through the carpeted living room where they grew faint and far, and then back to the kitchen.

"Probably my wife," I said, "getting a glass of water." Then, I heard the back door open. The footsteps stopped over our heads. I heard her voice call my name.

"Wally?" It sounded muffled coming through the floorboards.

"Down here," I called. "Down the back stairs." I thumped the floorboards above me with the flashlight. TinyTina was looking up with a worried expression. The creak of the back door was followed by footsteps coming down, with the loose riser clunking. I'd left the cellar door open, and my wife appeared, a small woman in plaid flannel jammies, sporting the punkish hairdo she could still pull off. I was about to introduce them, when my wife said, "Tina—What are you doing down here? My wife looked at me. I shrugged. She explained, "She's been coming to my library."

She returned her attentions to the girl. "I had my suspicions, Tina, but I didn't feel it was time to say anything yet."

The girl's eyes bugged out. "You're Cora, the librarian—oh my God." And she started crying. My wife immediately went to her and crouched down to give her a hug, right there on the dirty floor.

CORA TOOK OVER immediately. Within fifteen minutes, after what I suppose was a necessary interval of crying and hugs, TinyTina was in our shower, and her clothes were in our washing machine, under my supervision. Later, Cora came back to my service porch to help sort and fold, while a much less defiant Tina hovered in the background wearing my wife's spare pajamas. Cora assigned me to my service porch for a while longer, while she settled Tina onto our sofa.

"I'll come back and get you when she's asleep. I need to talk with her a little first, privately."

So, I settled back into my chair and pulled one of my books off of the shelf. It was an anthology of Russian short stories, some predictably dreary, some wry, most of them quite long. I finished two of the shorter ones, listening to the night sounds of the building while I read, and I was just getting started on a third, when Cora tapped on the door and slipped in. "She's sleeping. I'll take the day off tomorrow and see if I can convince her to try an agency."

"What happened to her at home?"

"She won't say. I imagine the worst, of course, but sometimes it's an accumulation of trivial things. Her clothes are nice. I think she comes from money. She has cash too. She shouldn't be out there." Cora stood small and straight in my little gray refuge. "How did you know she was in the basement?"

"I could hear something through the floor. After four nights of it, I had to check. I was expecting some old alchy, or maybe a punk."

"Well, you may have saved her from a lot of distress. Come to bed. It's already one in the morning."

I took my shoes off so as not to wake Tina, as we slouched through the living room. My footsteps nevertheless sounded loud as we passed her, wrapped in blankets on our sofa. As I lay in bed next to Cora, who could fall asleep almost instantly, I heard footsteps through the ceiling. The old man upstairs, Mr. Jeffers, couldn't sleep. Step, step, and the creak of a floorboard. The sounds of our little village in a box. After a while, I got out of bed and tiptoed back to my service porch. I sat down in my chair and listened to old Mr. Jeffers pace, while I finished reading the story. By then, my feet had begun to feel the cold. I tiptoed back to bed, trying not to let my footsteps give me away.

Bradley R. Strahan

THE ENDS OF EMPIRE

What wine was it that Alexander drank
in the passes of Hindu-Kush?
What song echoes back drunk centuries later?

All the centuries keep turning back
on themselves, ends and beginnings
endlessly knotting together

while we keep writing and rewriting
the same lullaby that no one will sing, as we
walk the line between love and treason.

And all the lies that ever were told
are tied to our legs like millstones,
while the beast of centuries circles us:

like Custer's Indians, like the fall of Rome,
like Alexander drinking himself to death
in all the plundered palaces of Asia.

So let Alexander sleep. His armies are toys
in the hands of children, tin soldiers
force-marched across a carpet of stones.

After all there is always wine,
wine and sleep, and children's voices singing.
Nothing changes those voices, nothing.

Diego Luis
PROCESSION TO OSHUN
MATANZAS, CUBA 2019

Andrew Ross

A STORY OUT OF THE BIAFRAN WAR

IN THOSE DAYS I SLEPT in the Park. When it was warm, I slept out on the grass, and when it was cold I slept, wrapped up in the white man's newspapers—the white man's lies—to keep myself warm, beneath the trees. At night, when the people went and the Park was locked up, I was all alone. Then, I was free to do as I liked. I could piss in the Serpentine, or I could take off my shoes and socks and walk barefooted. There was nobody to come tell me, "Hey, don't you know you can't do that here?"

I went to school in Nigeria for fifteen years, until I was twenty years old. Then, to learn everything the white man knows about the way this world is, which I knew I could not learn from books or at school, I left University and boarded a freighter sailing out of the Gold Coast for Liverpool. I wanted to see the white man's world with my own eyes and not merely to believe the lies he told me. I sailed back and forth along that route for four months, until I had earned enough money, and then I jumped ship in port at Liverpool. With my money, I took a train to London. I didn't want to go back to University, even though my father in Owerri had agreed to pay my fees, and I didn't want to get any damn work being paid shillings for cleaning up the white man's dirt. As long as I was out of work, I got paid something by the government dole. That was all I needed, if I lived in the Park

It was spring in 1964, and London was filling up with foreigners. German and Swedish girls came to take summer jobs, so that they might learn English. Italians and Greeks came to work in the cafes, and the Irish came to work at laboring jobs. Germans and Scandinavians and Australians and South Africans and large numbers of French and Americans came here for their holidays.

On Sunday, my friends and I would all go to the Speakers' Corner, where we would meet many of these new foreigners. Everyone came to see who might be speaking that afternoon. It might be the Kenyan boy who, instead of a shirt, wore nothing but a cloak of colobus monkey skins and would stand around shouting about Uhuru. It might be the Ghanian boy who read from Nkrumah's essays on colonialism, or an A.N.C. boy who could not go home after Sharpsville, or some Sudanese or Rhodesian or Malayan or Iraqi boy telling terrible stories of how he had been tortured by his government. The sun shone down, and the place was filled with tourists who were carrying cameras and bags, drinking cool drinks, and eating ice cream. We had learned to tell the different types of white people apart. Now, we could tell them apart without hearing them speak, but merely by observing their faces and clothes.

Most of my friends would go up to the girls that came to the Speakers' Corner. They would start to talk to them, hoping that they could persuade these girls to move with them. Most of my friends would do this, even those who were students here. They tried even harder, because they had found moving with a girl while they were studying here helped to ease the loneliness they felt in this unfriendly city.

A boy would approach a girl he could tell was an American, and he would say, "What is that camera you have there, Miss?"

She would answer that it was such-and-such a kind of camera, and she would act as if she wanted him to leave.

Then, he would say, "What do you think of that African man speaking over there?"

She would answer that she could not tell, that she didn't know enough about what he was speaking of.

Then, he would say, "But what do you think of the Africans here, Miss? You are an American, and I imagine that black men in your country are not like the black men here. I imagine you were surprised that a black man here looks you in the eye, that he can argue and discuss things with you intelligently."

And she would say that she had not talked to many black men here.

Then, he would say, "Would you like to come with me for something cold to drink? We can go right across the street there and get something at that café."

And she would say, "No thanks," that she had to be somewhere in a little while, and she should be leaving anyway right now.

Then, he would say, "Is it because you do not want to be seen with a black man? Is that why you refuse?"

And she would tell him that he shouldn't think that.

Then, he would say, "Because you know you are not in America now. You are a guest in this country now, and you will please behave like one."

Then, she would look very worried, because she was beginning to be afraid that he would do something to her. She would mention something about how he shouldn't accuse her of prejudice, because she had never been prejudiced.

Then, he would tell her, "You know, you people come here, and you bring your attitudes with you. Wherever you go as you are traveling around the world, you keep the same attitudes with you. Now, you are even killing yellow people in Vietnam, because everybody does not accept your ways. But we 'Third World' people, as you are calling us, believe in taking what we can get from the different people we meet and keeping an open mind. We will take from you some things, such as science and philosophy. Science is truth. There is not one Newton's Law for white people and one for colored people. But we will not take from you what you have done with this science and philosophy. We will not destroy the beauty of the world and enslave our fellow men. We will not take from you white people your lying ways, your deceit and your cunning, your worship of that great god of yours, money."

The girl would try to walk away, but he would clasp her wrist.

"Look at you!" he would say. "Do you think that I will try to hurt you? Do you think that a black man does not know how to treat a woman? I will tell you one thing. We may hate all of you white people for what you have done to us, and for the ways in which you have deceived us, but we believe in love, and we believe that a man may love a woman no matter who she is, and because of that we respect all women no matter where they may come from."

She would become even more anxious and would start to look around for help. Then, she would break away from his grasp, and that is how it would end.

It was a hopeless pastime, though I used to do it with the others. I was moving with white girls instead of moving with my own people, the West Indian girls and the few African and black Latin American girls who were there in London studying. And then, I loved one white girl, and I learned that you cannot, because it can only bring unhappiness.

IN THE SPRING, I MET an American girl at a party that was a being given by my friend Kenneth, a Nigerian boy. This was before the summer holidays, so I was surprised to see an American girl there.

It turned out that she was a student. She was living in London, studying painting.

Her skin was very pale where it was not tanned, as white as ours was black, and her hair was yellow and worn tied up in a twist. Her eyes were wide and pale as a cat's. She was learning to dance the Highlife, which is one of our African dances, and the boy who was teaching it to her was Kenneth, who at the time had just come back from studying in the Soviet Union. He had brought back with him many bottles of Russian and Polish vodka, which he carried with him to the party. All of us had drunk too much of it. I was very drunk. I felt angry, and when I saw this white girl among us dancing our own dance, I went up to her and said a stupid thing. I said, "You must take off that girdle, which our own women do not wear, before you can dance that dance properly."

Kenneth said, "You are too drunk my friend. She is dancing it very well. Why don't you leave her alone and sit down on that couch?"

But this girl was very attractive, and now I did not want to leave her.

I said, "I will go sit down on the couch if this girl will come with me," and while I was saying this, I clasped her wrist. She did not try to pull away from me. She merely looked at Kenneth.

Then, she turned around and went with me to sit down on the couch.

"Why did you come with me over to this couch?" I asked her.

She did not answer me.

She slipped down further and further, like a cat, until she was practically lying on her back.

"You are not afraid of a black boy like me?" I said.

She shook her head.

I was wrong about this girl. I should not have paid any attention to her, but I kissed her, and she didn't push me away. She held me around the neck with her arms. So, I said, "You will kiss and hug a black boy, but will you come into the back room with him?"

And she said to me, "All right." And then, we went into the back room.

I thought to myself, Now, will this girl ever speak lies or think lies? Those were not things she would do, I learned later. Her lying would be in the way in which she acted, and she was helpless to stop that kind of lying.

On the next day, I rang Kenneth to ask him about the girl.

"Who was that American girl?" I asked him.

"Robin? I would advise you to keep away from her," he answered. "She is a hopeless person. She will only cause you unhappiness. I know what I am talking about, because that is what Robin did to me."

I did not see the girl for several days, until one night she appeared in the Park, as I was preparing to go to bed.

"Why did you come here?" I asked her.

She said, "Because I wanted to see you again."

I told her what Kenneth had said of her.

"Kenneth doesn't understand me," she said.

I told her I thought she didn't understand herself.

"That's not what I meant," she said. "Kenneth doesn't understand what I want."

I told her that I was not like Kenneth.

Then, she said, "The Park's locked for the night. Can I stay here?"

"You have planned very well, my dear," I told her.

"I brought my own newspaper," she said, and she took a copy of the *Paris Herald Tribune* from her bag.

I was pleased that she had looked for me.

That is how we began to move together. She was eighteen, and she had come from New York to study painting in London, in spite of the fact that her parents did not wish her to do this. This was something a girl in my country would never do, to disobey the wishes of her elders, but Robin had been doing this for several years now. The summer she was sixteen, she had wanted to go to Mississippi to help the American blacks there to vote, but her parents had forbidden that. The next year, when she was seventeen, President Kennedy was assassinated, and she refused to go a memorial held by her school for him. She said that, though it was terrible that he had died, she could not mourn him like a saint. She would remember children killed by bombs in Birmingham or in civil war in Brazzaville or by hunger in Tehran, but not that man.

Her teachers held a meeting, and it was decided that she did not have to go, but that she must produce something as schoolwork to express what she felt.

She painted a picture of a golden bird sitting on a tree above a landscape of city and countryside, and on the tree were dying purple flowers that were dropping down. The painting hung in the entrance hall and was a great success.

When I asked her whether her parents were angry with her for coming to London, she said, "Oh no," that they were hurt, but they were not angry. So, I asked how could she allow herself to hurt her parents in that way, and she answered that her parents didn't understand her. I told her that she wasn't very hard to understand, and she asked me to tell her what was wrong with her then. I told her there was nothing wrong with her, that she was merely a strange girl who did not mind behaving differently from everyone else. I told her that I had never known a white girl like her. It was much easier for a person to move with her than with other white girls, and as a result, she would be much happier than other white girls. She said that she didn't think that she was very happy, and I said that it was my duty to make her happy, as long as she was moving with me.

I should have remembered what Kenneth had said about her.

For three nights, we slept together in the Park. Then, on the fourth night, she did not appear. Then, I remembered what Kenneth had said about her. I thought to myself, she has left me, and I am a fool for believing that it would not happen.

The next morning, as I was leaving the Park, she was there, standing by the gate with her school books in her arms.

I said, "Well, Robin, you know you really could have told me you were not coming to the Park last night."

"I couldn't stand it anymore. There were too many insects."

I was so angry with her that I was about to walk away from her without saying anything further.

"I'm sorry," she said. "Could we sleep in my house?"

Hers was a lodging in Bloomsbury. She had shared it with another girl who was studying painting, but this girl had gone back to America. I agreed to stay with her there, and she was very happy about this. We slept on a mattress in the kitchen, because the other room was filled with canvases and boxes containing tubes of oil paint.

Each morning, she would go to school, and I would spend the day with a friend from the Congo, from whom I was then trying to learn French. In the evening, she would return from school and would cook us a meal, and then she would paint while I watched her television. I was glad I had come. To be truthful, it was almost autumn, and it would have been quite cold sleeping in the Park. On the wall of the kitchen, I taped up a photograph of Patrice Lumumba given to me by the Congolese boy, so that I would not forget the great changes that were now sweeping Africa and everywhere in the world, where the white man ruled. The Third World was a giant that lay sleeping, waiting for its moment, and now that moment had suddenly come with a pen stroke, or perhaps at the end of a Kalashnikov.

This arrangement was satisfactory for both of us. We were both very happy being in each other's company, and at the end of three months of living in this way, I realized that I had grown very much in love with her. I could no longer imagine leaving her. I could not imagine her completing art school and going back to America, and so, in order that I might have her always with me, I asked her to marry me. I told her that I would find steady work and would go to school at night. When I told her this, she was very happy. She cooked us an especially fine supper, and after we had eaten, we went to see a film.

But later that night, she went down the hall to take a shower before going to bed, and after half an hour she had not yet returned. I got out of bed and found her in the bathroom. She was sitting on the rim of the bathtub and crying.

This was the first time I had ever seen a white woman cry. It was something I could not imagine. I did not know what things caused a white woman to cry, whether it would be the same things that caused myself and my people to cry, such as pain, or grief, or anger, or whether it would be something else.

"Why are you crying?" I asked.

"I was thinking," she said. "What will happen to me when I marry you? I mean, where will we go, and what will we do?"

I said, "There is no need to worry about that. I will take care of you."

Then, she said, "But I don't even know you. How do I know you won't leave me?"

"Look at me," I told her. "Do you really think that I would leave you?"

"But I don't know what it will be like when we're married," she said. "What if it changes? You know you can't be satisfied with some shitty little job driving trucks."

"We will go to Nigeria," I said.

"But how will I be able to live in Nigeria?" she asked. "I don't know how to speak Nigerian, and I don't know anything about the way people live there. I'll go crazy."

I said, "Well, you can begin by learning that there is no such thing as 'Nigerian'. We speak many languages there. I am an Ibo, and I speak Ibo, and Kenneth is a Yoruba, and he speaks Yoruba. You can learn the language. If I could learn your language, you can learn mine."

She said, "It isn't the same thing. You were brought up with English customs. I never knew anything about Nigeria until I met you."

"Listen," I told her, "You are mad. Do you think that I knew one damn thing about you people before I came and learned with my own eyes? I never was given a hand towards learning anything but lies. That is what your so-called educators and priests gave to us."

"Well, don't blame me,' she said. "I didn't make it that way."

She did not say anything more, as if she were trying to remember what we had been speaking about.

Then she said, "It's just that I'm scared, because I try to imagine what it will be like being married to you, and I can't."

"You are afraid of the unknown," I told her. "If we go to Nigeria, you will see how wrong you are. It isn't, after all, like you will be on another planet in another universe. We're all human beings. And don't worry about me, so long as you will not mind what kind of work I do, just so that I can earn enough money to feed us, and pay the rent, and buy us new clothes."

I reached out my hand and clasped her wrist, saying to her, "Come, Robin. Let's go to bed. We will make a fine Ibo out of you."

But I wondered. I was sure she was moving with me for all the reasons that girls have when they move with men—love, friendship, a similarity of outlook, but I wondered if there were not also in her head a picture of a kind of man it would be right to be moving with—the way it was right to help people to vote in Mississippi or to worry about starving kids in Tehran—and I was simply that man.

We still planned to be married. We told all of our friends about it, and we decided that Robin would go back to America to visit her parents, who were not happy to hear about the marriage. I knew that, even in America, a young girl did not marry without saying one word about it to her parents, but I knew also that this case was a different matter. I knew that my proposal to Robin was honest and an act of love, but her parents could not have understood this, because to them all African men were the same, wishing only to move with a white girl because it was something exciting, or to take money from them, or to be stimulated sexually in a new way, and wishing only to marry a white girl to show the world that now it could be done. Since the Slade School at which Robin was studying was closing for the summer holidays, she would leave soon. She would plead with her parents all summer long, and hopefully make them see that we truly loved each other, and in the end they would give their blessing. We decided, however, that with or without their blessing, when she returned at the end of the summer, we would get married.

I rang Kenneth to tell him what had happened, and all the while I was doing this, I was thinking about what he had told me and what he would say to me.

When I told him, he said, "Then I have misjudged her. You are a very fortunate man to have such a clever and beautiful wife. I would like to give a party for you two, in your honor."

When the night arrived, all of our friends gathered in Kenneth's flat. We drank gin and whiskey and vodka, and we danced all night in the hot small room with no breeze to keep us cool, because it was summer. Robin looked beautiful. She was wearing a white dress with sandals, and her hair was tied up in a twist. The way in which she was dressed, and the way in which she was dancing with everybody, made me very glad that I would soon have her as my wife.

But as she had more and more to drink, she became more and more strange to me. Her eyes grew wide, as if she were staring at something terrible. Loops of hair began falling down onto her neck, and she was dancing strangely, as if she could not stand up any more.

"Robin, do you want to go home?" I asked her.

She shook her head.

"You know, you look very tired, and you must leave for New York tomorrow afternoon," I said.

She shook her head again.

"All right," I said to her, and I walked away.

Later, while I was dancing, I looked around me, but I did not see Robin. Almost all of the lights in the room had been turned off, and so I went into the next room, but still I did not see her. Thinking that she must be in the back room, I opened the door and went in. The back room was completely dark. I could see nothing. Then, I heard Robin laughing.

"All right, Robin," I said. "I want to go home."

I walked across the room, over to where the curtains had been drawn across the window. She was standing there, leaning against the curtains.

"I have to get my sandals," she said, but she did not move from where she was standing.

That is when I saw that her dress was completely unbuttoned down the front.

"Robin," I said. And a boy came out of the dark towards me, and I saw that it was Kenneth.

"You Cain," I said.

Robin still did not move from where she was standing.

"Come here," I said. "Let me turn the light on."

"Don't turn the light on," he said.

"Come here," I said. "How could you do this?"

I reached out my hand and clasped Kenneth's shirt at the neck. I pulled him towards me. He stumbled, and the buttons on his shirt flew off. Now, I was so angry that I brought the back of my hand up as hard as I could and hit him across the face.

"You Cain," I said again. "I'm going to kill you."

Suddenly, I realized what kind of a man I was about to let myself become, and all the anger in me turned to water, as my eyes filled up with tears. I let both my hands drop to my sides.

"What am I doing?" I said. "What am I doing? I don't want to hit you, Kenneth. Please just go away."

But he was already gone. I became angry once more. I felt so helpless and so lonely this time that I did not even have the strength to lift my hands.

"I never should have trusted a white girl," I shouted. "All of these white bitches are the same."

Robin was still standing in front of the curtains. I turned towards her and said, "Do you understand what you saw here just now?"

She nodded.

"You have almost succeeded in destroying me, but I am not going to become like one of you yet," I told her. "Thank God I still have enough strength in me that I can keep from becoming like one of you."

"I'm sorry," she said, and I could see that she really was sorry. "I'm sorry," she said again, and she started to cry.

I said, "I am not going to forgive you. You know that in one act you have hurt me, Kenneth, and yourself. A person who will do a thing like that is hopeless. You will do the same thing again and again for as long as you live. There is nothing else to say to someone like you."

I turned away from her and walked out of the room. I passed Kenneth, but I had so little strength in me that I could not even open my lips to speak to him, and so I walked out of the flat and out of the building. I walked to Robin's flat, where I lay down on the mattress and fell asleep.

When I awoke the next morning, I found that Robin had not returned. Her packed suitcases were still standing where she had left them the evening before.

I wrote a note for her. I told her that I was leaving the key and that I would not be coming back to her flat. I said that I hoped she would have a happy visit in America.

IN THE WANING WEEKS of 1964, I got a job at the London School of Economics as a research assistant, an opportunity I availed myself of, indeed. During that time, I perfected my English and felt more at peace with myself in the Green and Pleasant Land. My manners, my speech, the face I presented to the world, which I would mold into an English face to serve the calculated needs of the day and would then happily smash back into its constituent clay at the day's end, more and more took on that alien mode of their own will, and for longer and longer periods of time. For better or worse, I was turning into a black Englishman, and I minded not in the least.

Now, I felt differently about my academic career. I was weary of living rough, trying to discover the truth of the white man's world from the lower rungs. I wanted to go home and learn the truth of my own future from the top. I returned to Lagos and finished my degree in economics. I was first in my class. I made peace with my father, who was ill and having difficulty with his labors at the Cocoa Board. I began work on my doctorate.

I married Miss Diana Kinako. Her father, Hugh Kinako, was a glittering luminary in the Ministry of Oil. He had many friends and many contacts with foreign companies—Archer Daniels, Dow, Unilever Royal. Everyone likes to have a *kaffir* on the in-country team. There would be jobs for the asking, once I had completed my doctorate. We had a daughter, and Hugh bought us a home and a Toyota Land cruiser, and he gave me his cast-off Mercedes. We holidayed in Paris and the Canary Islands. Then, Diana caught me *in flagrante* with her cousin Hillary. Things got chilly.

I took a one-year Fellowship in Agrarian Planning at the University of California at Davis. In America, I made some attempt to look up Robin. I located her parents, who sounded most unhappy. Like me, she had married and had a child, a little girl they said. They would speak to her to see if she wanted to be contacted. They sent me a message in California—she was in college in Boston and willing—but I never followed up on it. I had returned to Lagos in 1967, weeks after Biafra had declared its independence and the federal blockade began, the troops moving south.

Ibos evacuated Lagos, and we all drove to my father's farm in Owerri, where we set up new, cramped living quarters. My doctoral work had, of course, ground to a halt. I was drafted into the Biafran Armed Forces and seconded to the Research and Development Directorate for work on a project that was to promote the growing of garden food plots all across the secessionist regions. Already, hunger abounded in the land.

By July, when the new capital at Enugu fell, I was moved to the airfield at Uli to coordinate the transport of the relief supplies that now were arriving from all over the world, as our dire situation increasingly made the headlines. It was depressing, thankless work. For each humanitarian flight allowed in, a dozen flights loaded with armaments and ordnance took priority. As the sustenance was offloaded, thieves stole off with sacks. Army Bedfords drove away with entire pallets. Finally, hungry locals shrieked and gibbered around the remaining stuff, until they were driven back with gunfire. All the while, well-fed mercenaries swaggered about, impatiently awaiting arrival of their own rations—cartons of Chivas Regal and Napoleon V.S.O.P.

We were sent on increasingly desperate and more primitive missions to grow food for the country, as famine encroached. There were Land Armies, troops of seed-sowing Boy Scouts, directives that looked pointless even on paper. By 1969, order was breaking down everywhere, and even our elite unit was barely getting enough food. Finally, communications broke down. Our little group of technocrats was left with nothing to do—and we were, by then, struggling to stay fed ourselves, reduced to theft and extortion. We lived in the bush, increasingly like wild men, hunting down rats and lizards with Sten guns. One day, in a dispute over whose wristwatch should be handed over to the neighborhood Syrian war profiteer for petrol, the C.O. machine-gunned his Sergeant. Those who wished deserted. We slept through the day and crept forth with nightfall, bartering our experimental seed stocks and equipment for the wherewithal of our continued survival. Occasionally, without the least sense of irony, we entered a local Red Cross food distribution center at gunpoint to carry off a couple of sacks of beans or rice, part of which we'd live on, the rest sell at exorbitant prices to the few who had any foreign currency, since our nation's own money was daily growing more worthless. We were shorn of ideals, illusions, allegiance, or affection for our country and cause.

In the autumn of 1969, with the nation shrunk to the land around Owerri and the airstrip at Uli, our little troop picked up a radio message from an Army headquarters near the front lines asking help in coordinating an exchange of prisoners with a federal unit operating nearby. Not daring to refuse, we were given the location of a meeting spot, where a few of us would proceed under a flag of truce.

As the third highest-ranking officer left, I was in the delegation.

We drove in our team's battered Morris Minor, a white cloth tied to its aerial, down murram roads, through devastated palm oil plantations. Heavy fighting had been happening. Along the roadside, one saw burned-out lorries and abandoned field artillery amidst piles of shell casings. As we neared the place, there were corpses—in our uniform, in their uniform, in no uniform—always eyeless, for the vultures ate those ready-to-hand gelatinous morsels first. They seemed to have been blinded by the fury of the terrible Armageddon they had witnessed. Or perhaps, like some tropical Oedipus, guilt had made them each scratch out their own eyes, which brought proof of their own complicity in the death of everyone's hope.

We came to a little bungalow—presumably once the plantation manager's office. A bomb had blown half its roof off, but purple bougainvillea still trailed gracefully across its white front wall, tinted saffron by the low morning sun. It was a moment of cosmic loveliness amid that human ugliness. Federal soldiers greeted us. We went inside, and there was a federal captain whose face and bearing stirred memories from the past. I had to think a moment—then I knew it was Kenneth.

"My God! Is it you?" I shouted.

He sported a ferocious beard now, as I did too, as did most of us who'd been living a furtive animal existence in the bush.

"You look like General Ojukwu," he said. "I didn't recognize you for a moment."

He smiled.

"And I barely recognize you. My God, things have changed. How long ago were we in England?"

"Four years ago."

"Incredible to think of it."

A federal sergeant looked at us sourly and muttered something to his associates. We began with the business at hand, the prisoner exchange.

"It's fortunate we could arrange this," Kenneth said. "In these parts, they've been shooting prisoners, you know."

"Well, we've been doing the same thing. So, there are no moral grounds for objection."

After going through most of the important issues—where the men were to be brought, the laying on of transport, notification of authorities on each side—a breather was taken for smoking and stretching. I sat beside Kenneth under the bungalow's iron porch roof. The day was balmy, with no hint of cordite, ashes, or carrion on the incoming breeze. I told Kenneth about my academic career, about Diana and my children, my important father-in-law, my hopes for an illustrious future, now perhaps rendered moot by the national struggle. In turn, Kenneth reviewed all that had happened in his life, since we'd been friends. He'd taken a degree in Modern Literature at St Andrew's University. He too had married, a Scottish girl, had produced two lovely and brilliant twins, and was now divorced. He missed his kids in the U.K. and went over to see them for holidays. When the war came, he'd been working for Nigerian Broadcasting, a safe job behind the lines in Lagos, but during the big counter-offensive in August, he'd finally been put in uniform.

"Biafra can't hold out much longer," Kenneth said. "Lagos is in for the kill. They're starting daylight strafing missions on markets and other public places."

He offered me a cigarette, a Dunhill Gold, which I hadn't seen in two years. I accepted, and he took one himself, sighing.

"In London, remember how certain we were about everything? We would borrow from Europeans, learn from them, but never be like them? God, what monsters of confidence we were."

I tried to remember myself, as I had been four years ago, how things had looked from within my head, but I couldn't. I could recall well enough the sights and people I'd seen, and then connect them with a memory of what I'd thought and felt, but it was as history long past. They were the thoughts and feelings of another person.

"What ever happened to that girl Robin?" asked Kenneth. "The one who swept you off your feet."

"And you off yours too, if I remember."

I told him what little I knew about Robin. How she'd married, had been attending university in Boston, and had herself produced a child. I didn't want to say that I'd had a chance to reach her but had never done so.

He smiled and blew away smoke.

"She found someone and is happy then. That was a hopeless girl."

Perhaps I was imagining it, but the wind seemed to shift just then, and now there was the smell of flesh in the air.

Michael Salcman

WHAT WE MEAN...

What we mean when we talk about love
is what we mean when we talk about war;

What we mean when we talk about war
is what we mean when we talk about peace;

What we mean when we talk about peace
is what we mean when we talk of salvation;

What we mean when we talk of salvation
is what we mean when we talk about love.

Rhema Sayers

THE VOYAGE

"DAD WANTS YOU at the boat, Ham."

Shem stood in the doorway of the large, rambling house. His younger brother was sitting at the kitchen table, scowling at a cup of coffee. He didn't say anything. Nor did he move.

"Ham," Shem repeated. "Get up and go to the boat."

Ham glanced at his brother. "Do you really believe that crap? Do you really believe what he says?"

Sighing, Shem leaned against the wall and regarded the teenager. Greasy, lank black hair fell over his dark eyes and pimply forehead. Now, that forehead was wrinkled with a frown, and the full lips were curled in a sneer.

"Our father has a life's calling, Ham. You know that. We are a part of a great…"

"A great pile of bullshit," Ham interrupted. "Our father is crazy, and everyone in town knows it." The boy stood. "And we're the children of the town psycho." He started pacing. "Do you have any idea of the kind of shit I have to put up with at school? Do you?" He was shouting. "I can't take it any longer."

He stopped in front of Shem and got right in his face. "Do you hear me? I…can't…take…it…any…more." With that, he stomped out of the room and slammed the door.

Shem sighed again. He glanced out the window at the rain. He had a feeling that Ham wouldn't have to 'take it' for much longer. The rain had started about ten days ago. Just sprinkles at first. Now, they were having showers every day. The roads were muddy bogs. But it was March. It always rained in March. Still he had the feeling that this was the Time. He had made his own preparations. Salit had accepted his marriage proposal. The wedding was to be held in three days. He could feel an urgency among the people, even among the animals, in the air. Yes. Definitely. It was the Time.

He watched Ham, trudging up the road, moving as slowly as he could, the slumped shoulders, taut hood, the whole body a statement of teenage resentment.

Shem couldn't help but smile. He'd gone through that stage, too. He'd hated his life, his family. He'd hated being the son of the laughingstock of the town. Resentful was not a strong enough word.

What caused him to believe, he didn't know. He just woke up one day with the certain belief—no, the certain knowledge—that his father was right. The floods were coming.

HAM REACHED THE SHIP, as Noah was stepping out on deck. His father yelled down to him. "Did you get that load of chicken feed from Elijah?"

Ham nodded, but his father couldn't see the movement with his hood pulled up, and he yelled the question again.

"Yeah, Dad. It came in. It's being loaded onto wagons now. They'll bring it up soon." He shuffled up the gangplank, carrying a bleating lamb. The foreman, David, had plunked it into his arms and told him to reunite it with its parents. He dropped the little one into the sheep pens and turned away. One of the workers called out. "Put that lamb in the right pen, numbskull. The number's on its tag."

His face grew hot at the rebuke, but Ham picked up the lamb again and looked at the tag. It said 23. He found pen #23 and placed the infant sheep inside. For a moment, he watched the obvious joy of the little family of sheep, as the lamb butted up against its mother's side and started nursing. The lamb was cute. He almost smiled.

Raising his eyes to the huge ship around him, he wondered for a moment longer. Maybe, just maybe, his father wasn't crazy. The rain was pelting the earth. Rivulets raced down from the mountain toward the town.

Then, he shook his head and pulled his hoodie back over his hair.

Noah looked down at the boy. He had seen something in him for a minute, but it was gone now, and the teenager was back. Well, it would come again at its own time.

SEATED AT HIS DESK in the captain's cabin two days later, Noah regarded the bills with despair. He had to pay them, but money was short. He leaned forward and buried his face in his hands.

Ham stepped into the cabin without knocking. He never bothered with the niceties. He saw his father sitting there, shoulders shaking, face in his hands, strangled noises coming from his throat. At first, Ham thought that his father was laughing. Then, he realized that the iron man, the man who never showed emotion, the stoic, was crying. He didn't know what to do. He began backing quietly out of the room, then stopped. He felt something break inside of him, as if a dam had burst. His eyes welled up, and the tears coursed down his cheeks. All of the anger, all of the resentment flowed out past that broken dam. It didn't disappear, not entirely, but the old man's grief overpowered his. He went to his father and put his arms around the man.

THE RAIN NEVER let up. It became a deluge, a wall of water. People in the town watched the creek rise and become a river, impassable, wild and straining at its banks. Then, the water broke out over the fields in the valley, flooding and destroying crops. Farmers hastened to move their cattle and sheep and goats to pastures higher up the mountain. They stared hard at the ark. Many in the town looked up toward the ship, though they couldn't see it through the rain. The water rose, and the rain never stopped.

Outlying homes on the lower slope flooded. Refugees moved in with friends and relatives. More than a few began to approach Noah. Some would forgive debts. Others could bring skills or fine animals as breeding stock. Some had nothing to offer except their belief—finally—that Noah was right. No one was turned away. A line began to form in the rain. Sodden people trooped up the gangplank to find quarters that were at least dry.

TWO WEEKS LATER, the water had risen above the first floor windows in the town. Noah leaned against the railing and stared at the line of people that disappeared into the rain. The debts were no longer a problem. Room. Room was the problem. Noah knew that there would never be enough room for all of them. Even now, they were approaching some invisible cut-off line. Unless—unless, he overloaded the ship. But that would put everyone's lives in danger.

He had been told not to take them all, that the flood was a punishment for sinners. *Who are the sinners, Lord?* he wondered. He was a sinner. Even Na'amah, his beautiful wife, was a sinner. Yes, the sins were minor. Coveting the neighbors' new carved mahogany table or her sister's jeweled hair comb. He remembered with shame, cheating on a test in school. He hadn't been caught, but now he rather wished he had been. No man or woman was perfect. Probably, when the Messiah came, he wouldn't be perfect, either. So how could he leave anyone, anyone at all, to drown? It was simple. He couldn't. They would just have to pack everyone in and pray.

Shem stood slightly behind his father and saw the toll that fate had taken on the man. He had a permanent slouch now, shoulders drooping, deep lines etched into his face. His eyes were the saddest Shem had ever seen. He felt a surge of pride in this man. Despite the never ending work, despite the way the ark had crippled his social life, despite the scorn and practical jokes he'd suffered through, he realized that he was lucky to have this man as his father.

Shem's shoulders straightened. He stepped forward. "Let me help them for a while, Dad. You go lie down and rest."

Noah didn't seem to hear him. Then, his eyes turned to his son, and he smiled. "Thank you, Shem. I think I'll do that." He shuffled up the gangplank.

DARKNESS WAS SETTLING upon the watery landscape, when Shem noticed a commotion. A large group of people were pushing their way forward through the line, shoving people, carts, and animals out of their way.

Shem was not surprised to see Aaron, the mayor of the town at the head of the band. There were at least fourteen or fifteen adults, numerous children, cats, dogs, and several wagons full of furniture, pots, pans, rugs, paintings, and vases. There was even a marble statue, for goodness' sake. Suddenly, Shem felt as weary as his father looked.

When Aaron and his clan finally reached the front of the line, Shem asked him, "What in the heck do you think you're doing, Aaron? You can't push your way up to the front." He waved a hand. "These people were here long before you. Now, get to the back of the line."

The mayor's mouth fell open. "You can't do that," he sputtered. "I'm the mayor." His chest puffed out like a bantam rooster's. "Now, look here. You just get out of the way, Shem. We'll find our own places." And he tried to shoulder Shem aside.

But Ham was there. And Japheth. And the mayor found himself blocked.

Ham motioned to some men behind him. "We'll handle this, Shem," he said, and they started to shepherd the raucous family back along the line.

The mayor screeched. "Where's Noah? I demand to speak to Noah. He'll set things right."

Noah's voice came from the captain's walk. "I think things are being set right, already." He gestured toward the town. "You're not the mayor any longer, Aaron. There isn't any town left."

They could hear Aaron's voice fading into the distance. "Get your hands off me. How dare you. What are you doing? I can pay. I'll pay whatever you want. Noah . . ."

But Noah had disappeared into the ship.

THE ARK FLOATED OFF ITS BLOCKS, as the last goat was herded aboard early in the morning. Even the mayor was aboard, grumbling continuously about how he was being treated, bedded down in the sheep pens. The marble statue had been left behind, along with the chairs and tables, and almost everything else. All the dogs and cats were on board, though.

The only sign of the town was the spire atop the temple.

As the great ship, overloaded as it was, made its way ponderously through the water, Ham caught sight of a shape clinging to the top of the tower. He couldn't tell what it was, but it was moving. He called to his father and pointed to the last refugee.

Noah called out his orders, and the ship began a slow turn to port.

"It's a damn cat. Don't stop for a damn cat. You'll get too close to the temple and wreck the boat." That was the mayor, of course.

"It's a ship, Aaron. Not a boat," replied Noah calmly. "And yes, we are going to pick up that damn cat. At this point, every life is precious."

The ark was on its maiden voyage, but Noah was an old sailor. Slowly, carefully, he maneuvered closer and closer to the temple and the cat. Shem grabbed a pole and held it out, but the pole just wasn't long enough. The cat looked at them and yowled. Yellow, with long sodden fur, the animal held on desperately.

Before Shem could say no, Ham was in the water and swimming to the tower. The ship moved in a circle, trying to stay away from the building. Nothing could be seen in the dark, gray water.

Ham reached the spire, and the cat jumped, digging its claws into his shirt and his scalp. Ham yelped, but he made no attempt to move the animal. He pushed off and started the swim back. Blood was running down into his eyes. The wind was pushing the ark away, and the gap between boy and boat was growing. Then, the current caught the boy, and he swirled away, moving faster than the ark, until he and the cat faded into the gray waters.

Shem jumped over the railing in an instant, but Ham had jumped even faster. As Shem climbed back, he felt the ship scrape along the roof of the temple. A low-pitched, drawn out shriek filled the air, and then, they were past the building.

The mayor was shouting imprecations at Noah, calling him incompetent. "I'm going to form a committee. We'll circulate a petition to have you removed as master of this vessel. You shouldn't be allowed to captain a rowboat . . ." His voice trailed off, as several burly sailors led him back to his sheep pen.

They could do nothing but sail in the direction they thought Ham had gone. The charts were useless. The water wasn't especially cold, but Noah knew that Ham couldn't survive for long in water twenty or thirty degrees below his body temperature. They sailed with the current. The ship moved along well, despite her load.

Hours passed. The ship was quiet except for the creaking of the wood, the flap of the sails, and the occasional animal complaint. People stood on the decks, eyes searching. They said very little. The dim light that was the sun climbed high into the heavens and started its downward descent. Shem and Japheth stood near their father, unable to help him, unable to help themselves.

A cry came from above. "Something off the port bow. I can't make it out. But it's there."

The ark changed her direction, slightly. They waited.

Again, from above. "I think it's a human."

Another twenty minutes passed before they could see for themselves. A body lying in the water, face up. A tinier body on its chest.

Shem had a boat ready. Eight men rowed, sending the skiff flying across the water. When they reached him, Shem knew he was dead. His face was blue, his eyes closed. He reached down and grabbed Ham's shirt. The eyes opened. Shem almost dropped him.

"Ham? Ham!" Ham shook his head slightly and tried to smile. He picked up the cat and gave it to Japheth, as they hauled him aboard.

Once aboard, they stripped him bare and rubbed him dry. They wrapped him in blankets and put him to bed. Na'amah got some hot soup down him. Then, they let him sleep. Na'amah gave the cat to Shem's new wife, Salit. The cat was doing better than Ham. She had consumed a bowl of soup and was now wrapped up in her own blanket on Ham's cot.

Ham slept for almost two days. When he woke and tried to stand, Shem had to support him. Another day, and he was almost back to normal. The cat had refused to leave him during his recovery. Now, she went everywhere with him. He named her Sarah.

THE FIRST COUPLE OF WEEKS went by easily. The rain continued, but the winds were fair. The ark handled well, although a little sluggishly. They had to bail almost constantly; the rain was trying to drown them. There was enough food for everyone, even if the portions were not large. Na'amah said she'd finally found a diet that worked, and everyone had gotten over their seasickness. The mood was upbeat, if not happy.

They saw a patch of blue sky at the beginning of the third week, but it disappeared behind a towering wall of black thunderheads on the western horizon. By nightfall, they had to reef the sails, trimming back until she barely made headway against the storm. The ark wallowed up one side of a colossal wave and then plunged down the other, burying her bow in the dark water. Every time she came almost straight down the side of the wave, Ham was sure she'd plunge into the water and keep right on going, down to the depths. Yet somehow, she pulled herself up again with a great shriek of tortured wood.

All of the civilians and half the crew were vomiting. They lost a horse, a cow, and three sheep during the storm. Probably a few birds as well. Sarah had weathered the blow by hiding in Ham's shirt.

Two days later the storm had blown itself out, and the ark floated on a sea of glass. The rain had stopped, at least for a while. The sun was still obscured by high clouds, but it felt warm.

The ark looked like a death ship. People lay scattered about, sleeping wherever they had fallen. Noah slept in his chair on the bridge. Ham had the helm and was keeping the ship on a northerly tack. The breeze was fitful, coming and going, playing with the sails like a child hiding in the sheets.

Ham was enjoying himself as captain of the ship, until he saw the mayor come stomping across the deck with a dozen followers. He started to climb up to the bridge, but Ham spoke up. "That's far enough, Aaron. No civilians on the bridge."

"Don't you tell me what to do, you little weasel," the mayor snapped. "I'm taking over this boat, and you'd better get out of my way." He continued up the ladder.

Sarah hissed and spat at the mayor, while Ham looked at his father.

Noah was suddenly on his feet. He stepped to the head of the ladder and placed his boot on Aaron's hand.

The man screamed and yanked his hand away, nursing it to his chest. "Get out of the way, Noah. You're no longer captain of this boat."

"It's a ship, Aaron."

"I don't give a good goddam what you call it. I'm taking over, you incompetent fool."

Noah stared down at the red-faced mayor. "I don't think so, Aaron." He shook his head. "In fact, you and all of your followers are hereby placed under arrest."

Aaron's mouth fell open, and a laugh rolled out of it. He nearly fell off of the ladder. "You and what army are going to do the arresting, Noah?" He made a show of looking around the deck. "I don't see anyone trying to arrest us." He glanced back at his men, who were starting to look a little uncertain. Things weren't going the way they were supposed to. "Do you see anyone trying to arrest us?" he asked them.

When his gaze returned to the captain of the ark, he found himself looking at the pointy end of a very sharp spear. He backed down the ladder a step or two. "Now, Noah, we don't have to do this the hard way. Just take your boys, and back off. We'll let you have the first mate's cabin. Now, Noah, don't get excited. Noah—"

Noah was coming down the ladder, still facing the mayor. He held the spear pointed at the man's chest. He poked the mayor gently, and the man squealed and fell backwards onto the deck. Ham, Shem and Japheth leaped down to stand beside their father, each with a long knife.

Aaron scuttled backward to reach the safety of his men, before he climbed to his feet. He turned to his followers and shouted, "Take them. Throw them overboard." He shoved one man forward.

A couple of his followers pulled out knives, but one pushed through the group to face the mayor. "What about you, Mr. Mayor?" The words dripped with sarcasm. "Aren't you going to join us in this little skirmish? Or are you going to run and hide behind a hatch?" He looked at the others. "I'm going back to my quarters. Noah's a leader." He pushed the mayor hard enough that he fell. "This scum isn't." He walked away.

A moment later, several more followed him. Then, a few more. Finally, the mayor was left alone, crouching on the deck.

"What do you say, Dad? Throw him out to the sharks?" Ham smiled.

Noah snorted. "Get out of here, Aaron. Just go."

WEEKS DRAGGED BY. The winds were fair, but water still poured from the heavens. Everyone was hungry, and everyone was grumpy. The muttering from below decks was getting louder. Noah stood on the bridge and prayed. He refused to go to his cabin. Finally, he collapsed, and they carried him there. Shem took over, and the ark sailed on. Aaron would stride onto the deck at times and watch, eyes shuttered and the corners of his lips turned down. Then, one evening, Noah reappeared on the bridge. He still looked haggard, but somewhat better.

The next morning dawned clear and bright. The breeze was brisk, and everyone's mood improved, even if the food was almost gone. But still, no land that day, or the next, or the next.

Lack of food caused short tempers. They were down to quarter rations. Fights broke out. A lamb was slaughtered, and the family responsible was almost lynched. The mayor had started another rally. The sun was going down on another day.

"Land, ho!" came the cry.

And a raven came gliding in to land on the top mast.

THERE WERE THREE LARGE VOLCANIC ISLANDS, one with smoke rising from the peak. The largest had a lovely little harbor with a natural stone wharf. They brought the ark in and tied her to several huge trees. Then, they let the gangplank down, and the people poured out of the ship onto the land.

Almost before the last family had disembarked, Aaron was giving a speech, welcoming his people to this new land, as if it belonged to him. Most ignored him, but there were a number of men who coveted positions of power in this new country, and they clung to him.

Noah leaned against the railing and watched, as men and women moved from group to group.

Finally, a man named Zacharius stood up and challenged Aaron. He accused the mayor of being a cowardly, power-grabbing idiot who had endangered them several times during the voyage. All of this was true, of course. Aaron tried to reassert whatever authority he'd had, but it had eroded away. He was left yelling at the backs of the throng that was listening to Zacharius.

Aaron became enraged and, raising his voice, began pulling at people in a last effort to make them turn back to him. One powerfully built young man became annoyed and knocked the ex-mayor into a patch of thistles, where he thrashed about and cried for help to no avail.

Zacharius organized the people, and work began to build new homes.

HAM STOOD BY THE RAILING on the bridge. His father stood behind him. Ham had cheered when Aaron got knocked down, despite his father's reprimand. Now, he watched avidly, as Zacharius started organizing the people. He almost didn't notice when Noah's hand slipped from his shoulder, and the man fell quietly to the deck. Ham cried out, but Noah was gone, a smile still on his face.

Mary Shanley

BILLY FINGERS

Billy Fingers wore a black glove
with the fingers cut off on his right
hand. It was unusually street of him,
in his cashmere coat, collar always
turned up. Italian leather loafers.

Billy was a flappy guy, like
a newspaper, thin and full of stories.
Today, he spoke about using drugs
in a heroin salon; it was cut above
a shooting gallery, is what he said.
Maybe there were a few chairs
and a lamp hooked up to the
electrical wiring in the building.

Billy heard that if you are going to
overdose from a shot of heroin,
it will happen in the first minute
after the injection. So, Billy
would shoot up and then watch
the second hand go around
the sixty second cycle, and when
a minute passed, he felt that he
was safe, and relaxed into a dreamy,
dope nod.

Billy Fingers never appeared to work.
We were all curious as to what kind
of racket he had going on. He was
one slick cat, in his hand-tailored
suits and—always—the glove.

Maria finally learned that Billy's
family owned an apartment building
over on Jane Street, and Billy managed
three floors of the six. He jacked up
the prices and lived large off the
profits.

One day, he left for a trip
to Italy. He wanted to drive around
Tuscany; taking in the world-famous
paintings, frescoes, and sculpture.
He would enjoy the rolling hills and,
no doubt, he'd eat the finest cuisine
the countryside had to offer.

How would he survive without
his heroin salon? Billy is a savvy,
street-smart young man, who sniffs
out the places in cities where a junkie
can safely cop and get high.

No worries for Billy Fingers,
until the day he overdosed
and died. It happened more
than a minute after he shot up.
So much for junkie science.

Peter Smith

SCALENE

M{\scriptsize Y} {\scriptsize BEST} {\scriptsize FRIEND} {\scriptsize IN} {\scriptsize HIGH} {\scriptsize SCHOOL} was a scalene triangle. There were other triangles, but they didn't like me. So, I ignored them. There were equilateral triangles—triangles with three equal sides. These were adaptable, broad-minded triangles. They showed the same side to everybody, regardless of whether they really liked them, but that was only for show. In reality, if they didn't like you, they smiled and went their own way. There were also isosceles triangles, which had two sides the same and one smaller side. They made no bones about not liking you and did it in a very sarcastic way to let you know you were inferior. They hung out with the equilaterals and the rights. The right triangles were probably the worst. They were from that Pythagoras genealogy, 'the squares of the sides,' and had a ninety degree angle, broad linebacker shoulders. They were obstinate, aloof, and athletic. They banded together and were loud and raucous. You could hear them at their table in the cafeteria, as you sat alone munching your sandwich. I ignored all of them, telling myself I could do without them. Deep down, that was a kind of defense mechanism. They would never approach me or want my company, so I sort of rejected them first, although I'd been semi-officially rejected in the cafeteria already, as well as in the gym and in the halls.

I liked the idea of the scalene triangle. I could relate to it. A scalene triangle has unequal sides and unequal angles. It is so unequal in everything that it encompasses all aspects of losers everywhere. It covers a broad swath of misfits who are gangly, awkward, and socially inept. The more I read about scalene triangles, the more I liked them and wondered if they were found in the real world, beyond my geometry book. One day at my table, I spotted another one. How did I know he was a scalene? Well, he looked like me and walked like an erector set collapsing. He approached my empty table and asked if he could sit down. I said 'okay,' but not with a whole lot of enthusiasm. Who knows. Maybe he was just a lost isosceles. We talked a little. It turned out he had weird thoughts. I had weird thoughts, too. I kept a catalog of them. The next day we talked a little more. He was quiet, but like I say, he had ideas. I had ideas about everything, too. Was revolt possible in a permissive society? Is human nature something people describe to explain their weaknesses? Are there many ways to be clever, but only one way to be sincere? We talked about that. Soon, other scalenes found our table and sat down. We all talked. Then, we needed more tables. We slid several of them across the linoleum cafeteria floor, so that they connected lengthwise. More scalenes found us, and our table got noisy, almost unruly. We weren't exactly like the rights, shouting with mouthfuls of food about how we won football games, but we had lots to talk about—the atom, the universe, how morality is what you wind up with after you screw a lot of people and then get caught.

Eventually, an equilateral couldn't get a seat at his regular table, wandered over, and asked to sit with us. This was a first. It had not happened before. All of us had personalities that had been pressed into the contour of accommodation, so we were inclined to say 'yes,' but a funny thing happened. Now, the shoe was on the other foot. Here came an isosceles wanting our company for the first time. We formed a phalanx of silence that forced him to stand there in front of us and let us witness the spectacle of his isolation.

Not a word was spoken. He walked away. I don't know where he ate lunch. As soon as he was gone, we laughed harder than I can ever remember. I found something new to add to my list of weird thoughts—The need to exclude others you don't like is stronger than the need to include those you do like.

Eventually, of course, there was the opposite sex. She looked like a rhombus.

"Are you a rhombus?" I asked her one day in the hall.

"I'm a kite," she said. "We're like cousins. Rhombuses have four equal sides. I have two pairs of equal sides, sort of like a kite. I can fly." She spread her upper corners for me. I could picture her soaring somewhere, somewhere beyond the rainbow, and I could picture myself sailing with her.

"Let's have lunch," I said. And we did.

She was a misfit, a real clunker. She was awkward and long-limbed, with sharp, piercing eyes that searched for contradictions. Her brain had developed faster than the rest of her, which meant she said some really weird things. "Do mirages really exist?" she asked. She had theories of her own—"Maybe the reason God kicked Satan out of heaven was that He saw Satan was incapable of happiness."

We got along swell. After high school, we got married. It wasn't a big, fancy wedding, like when an isosceles marries a circle or a rectangle. A few friends in a church, a reception, and a honeymoon to Ulaanbaatar and the Gobi desert—standard stuff.

Then, we had kids, a bunch of them. We didn't know what they'd be like, and they were all different. We had equilateral, isoscelese, right, rhombus, another with three dimensions (a globe), one with five dimensions (an n-tuple or tesseract), and a couple more or less like us. We were forced to start rethinking things. A tesseract was something I could deal with, but an isosceles? Those were my adversaries once upon a time in study hall, on the bus, in the lunchroom. Now, one of them was our progeny, our offspring, with big eyes that blinked at me, begging me to pick him up and hold him. How could I hate anything as beautiful as he was? We don't know where any of this DNA came from, but Kitey (I call her Kitey) says that she had a great-grandfather who was a cubinder, the Cartesian product of two circles. Our kids are amazing and have journeyed all over the universe to see if it is expanding or contracting.

"It is," they tell us.

Then, our children had children, and they inhabited the outermost regions of the universe and populated the lesser known places, where mathematics and love converge and God is found in the mouths of the newborn.

We talk about them constantly but seldom get a visit. When one of them comes home for a week or a weekend, it is a cause for celebration, and there is a big meal with games afterward. When all the little ones are tuckered out, Kitey gives them baths to make sure they are fully pooped. Then, I put them to bed, and they scream for me to read to them. Kitey would like me to read *Mother Goose* or Doctor Seuss or *Mary Poppins*, but I have something else in mind.

I pull out my old geometry book and tell them about all the triangles, how wonderful they are but how different. Either the words from the book or the depth of my voice or the bath they got from Kitey makes their eyelids droop, and soon they are asleep, but not before telling me they can hear the ocean when they flush the toilet. I put the book down gently and exit the room for my own room. On the way, I pass a window, where I bid goodnight to the moon, the stars, the shadows cast upon the distant frustums and knotted projective planes, and I go to sleep myself, dreaming of Archimedes and the fulcrum he imagined that could lift the world if it were long enough.

Don Stoll

WHITE

Sylvain and Ellen were unprepared to get stuck in a pothole. Darkness approached in the bush as swiftly as the lion they'd seen kill a zebra that morning.

"We're literally in the middle of sodding nowhere," Ellen said.

"Better thumb it," Sylvain said, thinking that she'd misused "literally."

Ellen rolled up one leg of her khakis. "It Happened One Night," she said.

"Unfair," he said.

"Mustn't be unfair," she said.

She rolled her trouser leg down.

"When's the last time we saw another car?" she said.

They'd congratulated themselves on their willingness to drive to the most remote parts of Kenya for animal viewing. Now, they thought they might have done better to stay on the beaten path.

"No clue where we are," she said, climbing onto the Land Rover's bonnet. "Could be Côte d'Ivoire. Your gran in that valley has fried plantains and avocado soup for us."

They still planned to fly from Nairobi to Côte d'Ivoire after finishing their safari. They planned to visit Sylvain's birthplace.

"More likely Uganda," he said. "Idi Amin would love you."

"Don't think we're four hundred miles lost. Smoke from cooking fires to the west."

She jumped down.

"Sun's in our eyes if a lion attacks," she said. "But westward ho anyway."

Sylvain had no pertinent answer when Ellen, realizing that her joke needed to be taken seriously, asked "What if a lion does attack?"

"Stay in the Land Rover overnight?" he said. "I know how we can keep warm."

"Tempted," Ellen sighed. "But we'll starve. Better hoof it."

As they walked, they examined a variety of approaches to dealing with a lion.

"Can't arrest it?" he said.

"No jurisdiction here." Ellen was a Detective Inspector with London's Metropolitan Police. "Can't offer your services in exchange for our lives?" she said.

"King of the jungle quite pleased with its appearance, my understanding." Sylvain was a cosmetic surgeon.

AFTER WALKING FOR THIRTY MINUTES, they found themselves in the only café in the village of Ngula. Almost the first thing Sylvain had learned to say in Swahili, after "Hello" and "Where is the toilet, please?" was "I'm not African; I'm French." Now, when the man closing the café because the daylight had gone spoke to him, he said, "Mimi si Mwafrika; Mimi ni Mfaransa."

The man also knew some English. He explained that he had no beer left, only Coca-Cola. Ellen drank one, and Sylvain drank one.

Then, he led them to the home of a man named Ibrahim, who had a wife and six children. Ibrahim's family spoke not a word of English. They smiled without ceasing, as they invited Sylvain and Ellen inside.

The guests ate a hot dinner of rice, beans, and tea. They were never told the wife's name, but they memorized the names of the children.

The café man said Ibrahim made furniture. So that he could work during the rainy season, he'd attached a shed to his house. This was the dry season. The shed was empty.

"Suppose we'll sleep out there," Sylvain said.

"Nothing to lie down on," Ellen said, "but it's not cold."

With her fingers, Ibrahim's wife had given the age of the youngest child, Shakila, as two. The little girl became sleepy. The mother and all of her children went out to the shed. Ibrahim led his guests into the only bedroom. Sylvain and Ellen tried by means of gestures to insist that they should take the shed. Ibrahim insisted more strongly that they shouldn't.

They lay talking quietly on the bed that Ibrahim and his wife had given up. They wondered about the time. Sylvain dug his watch out of his backpack. Ten o'clock. He reached beneath Ellen's t-shirt. She intercepted his hand.

"Shed's other side of that wall," she said.

AFTER A HOT BREAKFAST OF RICE, beans, and tea, Ibrahim introduced the foreigners to his neighbor. Paul Nimokate was an older man and a schoolteacher. He spoke English.

"Can you tell us the name of Ibrahim's wife?" Ellen asked.

"Mrs. Abdi," Paul said. "She is the wife of Ibrahim Abdi."

Paul and Ibrahim talked at length. Paul finally spoke to Sylvain and Ellen.

"Ibrahim is worried about his friend, a certain Timothy."

Paul and Ibrahim talked again for a long time.

"Ibrahim will find some men who can help with your Land Rover," Paul said. "We will go to see Timothy."

Ibrahim shook their hands.

"Come with me," Paul said.

"I think they want us to help this certain Timothy," Sylvain said to Ellen.

Sylvain told Paul that he and Ellen hadn't wished to see Ibrahim's large family relegated to his shed. Paul laughed.

"Ibrahim said that white people only know how to sleep on a bed," he said.

TIMOTHY'S APPEARANCE startled Ellen.

"You can see this boy is albino," Paul said, as the young man shook hands with the foreigners and smiled.

Ellen tried to imagine Timothy's features sheathed in dark skin.

"You understand the danger?" Paul said.

"When we were at—"

"In the lodge," Sylvain said, interrupting his wife. "On the news."

They didn't want to repeat the story in front of Timothy. Near the border with Tanzania, an albino man had been beaten to death for his body parts in front of his children. Another man, not an albino, had tried to intervene. The Good Samaritan was also beaten to death. The children were young, but on the basis of their statements, the police were looking for a group of four men in a large white car.

"Everyone in Ngula hopes that Timothy can find a wife here," Paul said. "Here, he is safe because he is known, but not in other places."

"My wife and I also hope you find a wife here," Sylvain said, and then, to Paul, "Does he understand English?"

"He is shy to speak English, but he understands," Paul said.

He cleared his throat.

"He has already found a wife here, but there is a problem."

"Here it comes," Ellen whispered.

"The young woman is a teacher," Paul continued. "A certain Stella Ntutu. She is a colleague of mine. She was posted to this village from her home, which is far away."

He paused.

"The children love her."

"What's the bit you don't want to tell us, Paul?" Ellen said.

Paul took a breath.

"Marriage is impossible, unless the parents have been consulted," he said. "But Miss Stella's father is not well to travel."

"Timothy hopes we'll drive him to see Stella's parents," Sylvain said.

"After the men have removed your Land Rover from the pothole," Paul said.

Sylvain looked at his wife.

"We'll do it," she said. "Is it far?"

"The distance is not one hundred kilometers," Paul said. "It is close to Tanzania. Far for this boy, but not for white people."

"Is it close to where the albino chap was," Ellen said.

"Timothy can stay in the Land Rover with the window up," Paul said quickly. "People will think there are three white people. He promises not to get out of the Land Rover, even to help himself."

"Brave chap," Sylvain smiled. "Won't pee the whole way."

"Three white people will be safe," Paul said. "Even bad men are afraid of what your government will do if they kill white people."

Neither Sylvain nor Ellen had noticed the overnight bag sitting in the grass behind Timothy. Now, Sylvain picked up the dirt-colored bag.

"Shall we find your Land Rover?" Paul said. "We can help if the men that Ibrahim has found aren't enough."

Ellen allowed the Africans to walk ahead. Sylvain fell behind with her.

"If Timothy ever moves away," Ellen whispered, "he should wear blackface."

"Freaking hell, Ellen," Sylvain said.

IBRAHIM'S MEN HAD EXTRACTED the Land Rover from the pothole.

"Should we give them money?" Ellen asked Paul.

"Your kindness is their payment," he said.

Sylvain gave the men money.

"I don't know where we're going," he said.

"Timothy knows," Paul said. He became serious. "Jesus will not forget that you have performed this kindness."

One of the Africans spoke.

"This Muslim boy says God is with those who are of service to others," Paul said.

THE TRAVELERS WERE ALONE in the Land Rover. Sylvain started the engine.

"Got to help myself," Ellen said as she unbuckled.

The trees may have been fifty meters away. She took a few steps toward them. She looked back at the Land Rover. The men had turned their heads. Seen in profile through the dusty window, Timothy's face looked white.

"That was fast," Sylvain said, when Ellen returned.

"Not much there," she shrugged.

Sylvain didn't want to repeat the mistake that had put them into the pothole in the first place.

"Fly over the potholes like a bird," he said. "Move like a lion, and you'll be caught."

He laughed.

"The lion is powerful like the Land Rover, and this makes him proud, but trapped in a hole beneath the surface of the earth, he is prey to the Maasai."

"Fasten your seatbelt. It's going to be a bumpy ride," Ellen said to Timothy.

After a while, she spoke to Sylvain again.

"Open up the top?"

"You're crazy," he smiled.

He stopped. The three of them opened the top, and Sylvain drove again. Timothy remained seated, while Ellen—boots off—stood on her seat.

"I love Africa," she shouted.

She glanced down at Timothy.

"Sorry," she said.

Gradually, they left behind the isolation that had enveloped Ngula. Ellen was exposed to the dust clouds kicked up by passing vehicles. She endured the dust, because opening the top had been her idea. Finally, it became too much.

"Bloody hell," Sylvain said, as she sat down beside him. "Like you're part of that tribe where the women coat themselves in mud."

She felt foolish for having been so stubborn, but she wasn't about to admit it.

"Think they use ochre and butter," she said casually.

She looked at Timothy over her shoulder.

"Hope he's watching. Can't be a straight shot."

"Got him in the rearview," Sylvain said. "Keeps pointing straight ahead."

She closed her eyes, as they approached a massive pothole. The Land Rover struck the earth on the far side, and her teeth rattled in her head.

She heard Timothy shouting, "Kushoto."

Sylvain glanced at the rearview mirror. Timothy didn't point.

"Left," Ellen said, in time for Sylvain to choose a direction at a fork in the road.

She looked over her shoulder at Timothy.

"Was half-guessing," she said, "but he's smiling. Got a lovely smile."

She was trying to convince herself. She wanted to imagine Timothy with black skin.

He gave fair warning ahead of the next fork. "Kulia."

Ellen turned around. She raised both of her hands.

"How far?" she said. She showed Timothy five fingers, then ten.

He showed ten.

She told Sylvain ten kilometers.

The sun was beginning to set. The Land Rover abruptly pitched to the left.

"Be fun changing this tire," Sylvain said.

"We have a jack?" Ellen said as she climbed out.

Sylvain searched.

"Should Timothy get out?" she said. "Take a bit of weight off?"

"No one to see him here anyway," Sylvain said. "Where'd the cars go?"

Ellen realized that since the last right fork there'd been no traffic.

"Lovely jack," Sylvain said. "Hoist a bloody AMX-30 tank with this."

He laughed and looked at Ellen.

"Help the French army run away."

She didn't hear. She was watching a white Land Rover come up from behind. It stopped parallel to them, and Ellen wondered where Timothy was.

"Mzungus," the driver said. "What are you doing here?"

Ellen tried to count the occupants of the Land Rover's shadowed interior.

"You are needing a shower," said a different man. "I can't see your white skin."

"White skin is pretty if it is washed," the driver laughed.

"She forgets how to wash," the other man said, also laughing. "We can help."

"Group of men in a big white car," Sylvain said quietly.

"Loads of big white cars about," she said, thinking something else.

"Jambo," Sylvain said.

Ellen thought that his false cheer wouldn't fool the men.

They climbed out.

Four, Ellen thought. And Timothy's hiding or run off.

The driver took a tire iron from the back of his Land Rover.

Run off, I hope, Ellen thought. Rape me, murder us both, steal our Land Rover. No need for Timothy to die too.

"We have only this, mzungu," the driver said.

"Can change your tire for you before I change ours," Sylvain said in that voice that didn't sound like him.

Ellen noticed the other vehicle's flat.

"African men know how to drive on flat tires," the driver said. He shrugged off Sylvain's offer.

The two men who hadn't spoken approached Sylvain and Ellen's Land Rover.

"Nothing in there," Ellen said.

She worried that, by making her voice loud, she'd amplified the sound of her fear.

"They don't know English," said the one who'd laughed about washing her off.

He went to stand with the others, next to the Land Rover. He was the smallest of the men. All were smaller than Sylvain, but he wasn't a fighter. They were four, and she and Sylvain were two.

The four men looked through the rolled-up windows that were to have protected Timothy. Ellen thought she heard one of them say *gonjwa*. She'd learned the word for "sick" in preparation for their trip.

"You have some sick man?" the driver said.

A cough erupted from inside the Land Rover. It was ugly, like a smoker's cough.

The driver joined his friends. Ellen and Sylvain followed. Timothy lay on his side, head and arms covered by his jacket.

"He's cold, and he has a rash on his face," Sylvain said.

The cough exploded again, louder and wetter this time. Timothy's head, still covered, moved slowly to the edge of his seat. He spat on the floor.

The men retreated and drove away. Timothy rolled down his window.

"Freaking brilliant, you are," Ellen said. "I mean, brilliant."

"Genius," Sylvain said.

"If Stella can't marry you, I will," Ellen said.

STELLA NTUTU'S PARENTS GAVE Timothy permission to marry their daughter. They said they worried for him, but Africa was changing. Soon, there would be no more bad men killing albinos. All Africans would be Christian, and there would be no more witchcraft.

They heated water for Ellen to pour over her head. They said she needed to wash so she would look like a white woman.

Mercury Marvin Sunderland

IF YOU PUT ONE (1) BEAN IN YOUR MOUTH

if you put one (1) bean in your mouth
it will grow.
in seventh grade my science teacher showed us all
how you could put it in for the beginning of a class period
and how it would live off your spit
and the warmth of your body heat.
at the end of the class a lot of us took ours out and they'd sprouted.

last week i left a cup of beans behind.
i'd put some of them in my mouth. sure
and i watched how much they'd grown.
i guess it all makes sense then
but some days you just have to leave it in a cup of water
and move on.

three beans have entered my mouth and grown.
my roommates call me jack and the beanstalk.
i guess that makes sense because i'd love to climb up and see
just how much my beans have grown.

so today i go for a climb.
there are many beanstalks in the ground.
it's just how it works around here
because right now my apartment is crawling with beanstalks.
i'm not the only one planting them in the ground.
so i climb

and i ignore the way my hands and feet are blistering.
i destroy my new pair of doc martens on the density of travel.
i haven't eaten since yesterday and my head is in the clouds
but all i can do is climb.

in christian ideology they say that god and
the angels are in the clouds.
i don't think they ever said that in the bible but
that's just what a lot of people believe.
my gods live on mount olympus
and my dead live underground.

i do not believe
in hell.
the underworld
is not the same as christian punishment.

so i climb.
i can see mount rainier
the same as when i cheered about it as a child.
my hands are freezing and
i've got goosebumps all over my skin.
the sky is high and mighty
and cold and of little oxygen.

just a month ago jupiter had a temper tantrum.
i was in seattle and
the sky was covered in lighting.
my family was having a massive house party then
and we had to direct everyone inside.

today the sky is clear.
during the school year i live in olympia
and it rains even more here than at home.
but today the sky is clear.
the only rain in the world comes from me.

the world is clear today
and i am the only raincloud.
and so i climb.
i think i have now passed where the clouds should be.
i can feel myself falling apart but
there is a disc of clouds above.
the sky is not clear.
everything has chosen to move out of reach.

and so i climb.
i reach the unreachable
and i feel my body tear apart into dust.
in christian ideology they say i am made of dust
just like every other human being.
but i am not dust.
i am of prometheus' clay.
that's why i stick together and make it
even though i want to crumble into nothing.

and so i pull myself up and i sit on a cloud.
i hear the thundering feet of giants
because one smells the blood of a grieving man.

some believe that bread is the body and wine is the blood.
i always thought that was gruesome
but i slice my arm carefully
and burn my offering.
this isn't the first time i've burnt belongings for the gods.

and so i walk
and the giant leaves me alone.
the bloodthirst of christianity is disturbing to me
but i've done what i can to pass.

and so i sit on a cloud
and i search for the tips of each beanstalk.
this is a forest of grief
and i am merely a tender of three.

i find the nearest beanstalk
and i fall.
my hands do everything they can to grip the leaves but
i am falling
falling
falling.

i land at the bottom but
i wish i could've gone down below.
i am not orpheus
and my friends are not eurydice.
as much as i want to climb i
can't see them ever again.

yesterday i attended the funeral for
one of my closest friends in the world.
this is the third consecutive time
one of my friends has died and
i'm just so tired of this.

if you put one (1) bean in your mouth
it will grow.
in seventh grade my science teacher showed us all
how you could put it in for the beginning of a class period
and how it would live off your spit
and the warmth of your body heat.
at the end of the class a lot of us took ours out and they'd sprouted.

Sacha Bissonette

THE WATER AROUND US

ON MY WORST DAYS, before Joshua makes it home, I run an ice cold bath. When the tub is full I lay submerged, dressed in my work clothes, until my heart is pounding on the inside of my chest and the cold water becomes increasingly unbearable. When I am done, I drain the tub, strip naked, and put my wet clothes in the dryer. I lay flat and still on our bathroom tiles until my head clears, and I hear his car pull up. I quickly go to my room and change for the evening. When Joshua walks through the front door, I'm usually there, anxiously waiting to see him, still a little cold.

In the seventh grade, the teacher let us pick our topics for our final presentations. I chose marine and freshwater life. I was very excited. I saw it as an opportunity for this otherwise timid, sheepish girl to really shine. It was my moment. I was up all night researching and rehearsing. The next morning I volunteered to go first, to set the bar. I started off slowly.

"Have you guys ever heard of the Umbridae fish from the family Actinopterygii? They are also known as mudminnows. There are two types of mudminnows: the eastern Umbra pygmaea and the central Umbra limi. When mudminnows are afraid and sense danger they bury themselves into mud and hide. Mudminnows you see, have evolved with a modified bladder that allows them to breathe in low-oxygen levels. Combined with their uncanny ability to play dead, mudminnows can hide for weeks and survive. They can even breathe outside of water."

It was going well. I had the class's attention. "Have you guys ever gone snorkeling? Coral is really cool. Did you know that because the design and make up of coral is so similar to our bones, we have used it for replacement grafts? To help us heal. Did you know that we destroy that same coral? That we have destroyed over twenty-five percent of known coral reefs as well. That we take from our ocean and lakes and give nothing back? Did you know this? That whales are found dead with plastic in their stomach. Did you know this? Do you know this!"

In my mind I had nailed the presentation, but I was pulled aside after class. My teacher understood and respected that I was passionate about marine and fresh water life but cautioned against turning an educational opportunity into a manic diatribe aimed at my fellow students.

That night the teacher called my house, and my Dad picked up. She encouraged him to foster and support my aquatic interests. He just nodded quietly.

JOSHUA AND I met at the aquarium.

Every Saturday I would break from my studies, pack a few snacks, take the red line to the downtown crossing, and walk the half mile to the New England Aquarium. After repeating this trip several Saturdays in a row, I thought it would be wise to get a membership. Members pay no entrance fee.

I would spend those days alone staring into the fabricated water world, day dreaming of having gills form under my fragile jawline and the bones in my legs and feet breaking into place, forming a sleek, beautiful fluke. I would watch as dedicated fish moved in and out of different schools with purpose, just to get turned around again. I wondered what we looked like to them, peering through not a looking glass but a transparent divider of our two worlds, related but different.

One Saturday, there was a guy sitting on a bench next to where I was standing. He, too, seemed entranced.

"What's your favorite part of all this?" I asked calmly, as to not disturb the residents.

A little surprised by my question, he turned around and looked me straight in the eyes. "I've always loved water…is the easy answer I guess. It's kind of funny. There is a neat little story being told here. See that big guy right there? He's a tiger shark, and they're apex predators. Left to ocean rules on a day where he was especially hungry, he would eat any one of the species of fish swimming around peacefully in here; but because one of us has studied him and knows when he's hungry, we can feed him to make sure he doesn't go on a killing spree in front us, and all the little children that come in here."

I sat down next to him and continued listening.

"So it's wonder, it's adventure, it's therapeutic, it's pretty. But it's a lie, a peaceful one."

Fourteen months later, Joshua proposed. He laughed, as he placed an aquamarine ring onto my cold finger.

THIS TIME, JOSHUA came home early. I don't remember too much. I woke up in our bed with a horrible headache, chilled to the bone. There was herbal tea steeping next to me. I had done my regular ritual bath, but this time as I lay on the cold tiles, I passed out. He tells me that when walked in he called for me throughout the house. He discovered me naked and ice to the touch. He started to call for help, but I came to. I was speaking, but in a state, mumbling about mermaids. He tells me that he picked me up and wrapped me tightly in a towel.

That night I told Joshua why I liked aquariums so much. He had never asked.

I REMEMBER WAKING FIRST that morning, as I always did. Our family cottage smelled like pine, like the forest around us. I was excited. First order of business. I flew through the old swinging doors and started running as fast as my little legs could manage down the broken steps to the dock. The lake was calm and quiet. I had left some hooked fishing line in the water overnight in an attempt to catch any creature that swam by. Excitedly, I pulled the line up and out of the lake. Nothing. No bait left, and no fish.

I moved on. I was good at finding frogs, something to fall back on when the fishing had failed. I knew how to trap frogs. I would let them go, and catch them all over again. That I was good at, maybe even better than at fishing. I skipped over to where the sand and the tall grass meet the lake. Where the frogs lived.

Bang. Three things happened very quickly. In what order, I can't remember. I heard the old cottage doors smash open with what could have only been my father's strength. Followed by a cry, a loud desperate cry starting from the bottom of his stomach, ending at the tips of his limbs and open jaw.

"Lilly come here," he howled.

It was too late. I saw her. Lying there motionless in a magenta gown, her skin pale and blue, and her ankles intertwined with weeds. My mother had gone to the lake at night, but the lake didn't take her. It spit her out.

When I lie there motionless in the tub or in the kitchen, I think of her. I wonder what it was like for her when she drowned. I heard your body goes numb to a point where all is painless. I hope that's true.

Was her mind clear and calm, as her limbs surrendered, and she stopped fighting. Maybe. Maybe, the pleasant moments she did have played before her, swimming and dancing like neon fish in a flipbook. I heard that does happen. I hope little me would be on every page of her book, trying to catch fish or frogs, running through the tall trees, hiding and seeking, my hands entangled in hair, falling limp as I fell asleep on her shoulder after one of our adventures. I hope I'm drawn, etched, tattooed into her mermaid soul to make up for the time she took away from me.

ON OUR FIRST YEAR anniversary, Joshua bought me an aquarium.

CONTRIBUTOR NOTES

EMILY ADAIR is a student in her junior year of the Online Professional and Creative Writing Degree at Central Washington University. Her published works include a short story entitled "Loved" that received 5th place in a writing competition when she was age 14 and a small book of poetry entitled *Revel* that was self-published at age 18. Since then, she mostly just fills journals with her ramblings for her own process and review.

FAIZ AHMAD is a final-year student pursuing his Bachelors-Masters in Biological Sciences, I.I.T. Madras. He believes in poetry as the ground of bewilderment, of amazement at simply "being." His poems have been published in *Salamander, Storm Cellar, Off the Coast, Anima*, and others.

ESSAM M. AL-JASSIM is a Saudi translator. He taught English for many years at Royal Commission schools in Al Jubail, Saudi Arabia. He received his bachelor's degree in Foreign Languages and Education from King Faisal University, Hofuf. His translations appear in a variety of online and print Arabic and English literary journals.

PAUL BAMBERGER received an M.F.A. in Creative Writing from the University of Massachusetts Writing Program. His most recent book is *On the Badlands of New Times* (Deerbrook Editions Press, 2018). He is also the author of *Down by the River* (Islington-Bryer Press, 1999), an earlier book of poetry.

SACHA BISSONNETTE is an Afro-Trinidadian, French Canadian short story writer from Ottawa, Canada. He is a reader for the *Wigleaf* top 50 series 2021 and recently participated in the poets-in-residence program at *Arc Poetry Magazine* with mentor Stevie Howell. He's now participating in the Diaspora Dialogue short form mentorship program with Makeda Silvera. He has appeared in *Wigleaf, Litro UK, Lunch Ticket, SmokeLong Quarterly*, the *Maine Review*, the *Emerson Review, Cease*, and *Cows*, among other places. His story "Glass Birds" was shortlisted for the *Masters Review* flash fiction prize and is a *Mythic Picnic* short fiction prize finalist. He has upcoming short fiction in *Sante Fe Writer's Project*. He is currently working on a short fiction anthology with the help of a National Canada Council for the Arts grant, an Ontario Arts Grant, and a Youth in Culture 2021 Ottawa Grant. He is nominated for *Best Small Fictions 2021*. He was longlisted for *Wigleaf Top 50 2021* and has recently been selected for the Writer's Union of Canada—BIPOC Writer's Connect mentorship. He loves film and comfort food and tweets @sjohnb9

RICHARD ALAN BUNCH is a three-time Pushcart Prize nominee and the author of several collections of poetry, including *Greatest Hits: 1970-2000* (Pudding House Publications, 2001); *Mystic Pizzazz and Tiger Lilies* (Infinity Publishing, 2016); and *Running for Daybreak* (Edwin Mellen Press, 2004). His poetry has appeared in *Windsor Review, Lalitamba, Poetry New Zealand*, the *Hurricane Review, Poem, Hawai'i Review, Many Mountains Moving, Xavier Review, Slant, Homestead Review, Dirigible, Haight Ashbury Literary Journal, West Wind Review, Comstock Review*, and the *Oregon Review*. His latest work is titled *Original Blend: New and Selected Poems* (Infinity Publishing, 2017). He resides with his family in Davis, California.

STEVE CARR lives in Richmond, Virginia and has had over 350 short stories published internationally in print and online magazines, literary journals, and anthologies, since June 2016. He is the author of five collections of short stories, including *Sand* (Clarendon House, 2018), *Rain* (Lulu.com, 2018), *Heat* (Czykmate Productions, 2018), *The Tales of Talker Knock* (Lulu.com, 2018), and *50 Short Stories: The Very Best of Steve Carr* (2020). His paranormal horror novel is *Redbird* (2019). His plays have been produced in several states throughout the U.S. He has been nominated for a Pushcart Prize twice. His Twitter handle is @carrsteven960. His website is https://www.stevecarr960.com/ He is on Facebook at https://www.facebook.com/steven.carr.35977

JEFFREY S. CHAPMAN is an Associate Professor of Creative Writing at Oakland University in Rochester, Michigan. He holds a Ph.D. in Creative Writing from the University of Utah and an M.F.A. from Sarah Lawrence College. Most recently, he has had prose and graphic short stories accepted by *South Dakota Review*, *Cutbank*, *Sonora Review*, and *Black Warrior Review*. He is a recipient of a Kresge Artist Fellowship and a Sustainable Arts Foundation Award.

HOLLY DAY is the author of *A Perfect Day for Semaphore* (Finishing Line Press, 2018), *In This Place, She Is Her Own* (Vegetarian Alcoholic Press, 2018), *A Wall to Protect Your Eyes* (Pski's Porch Publishing, 2018), *I'm in a Place Where Reason Went Missing* (Main Street Rag, 2018), and *The Yellow Dot of a Daisy* (Alien Buddha Press, 2018). Her needlepoint and beadwork have recently appeared on the covers of *Your Impossible Voice*, *Sinister Wisdom*, and *QWERTY Magazine*. In this issue, her piece "Vision" is composed of glass beads and nylon string mounted on foamcore.

JOE DE QUATTRO is an American fiction writer whose short stories have been published in *Beloit Fiction Journal*, the *Los Angeles Review*, and the *Carolina Quarterly*, among others. He lives in California.

TEJAN GREEN is a cross-genre writer, editor, and educator. Her work has been published or is forthcoming in *Platform Review*, the *Bookends Review*, and *Caribbean Writer*, among other publications.

MARLON HACLA is a programmer, writer, and photographer. His first book, *May Mga Dumadaang Anghel sa Parang* (Manila: National Commission for Culture and the Arts, 2010), was published as part of UBOD New Authors Series II. He is also the author of *Glossolalia* (High Chair, 2013) and two chapbooks, *Labing-anim na Liham ng Kataksilan* (2014) and *Melismas* (OOMPH Press, 2016). In 2017, he created the first Filipino robot poet, Estela Vadal, as a Twitter bot with the Twitter handle @estelavadal. He lives in Quezon City, Philippines with his cats.

CLAUDIA HINZ lives in Bend, Oregon. She graduated from Harvard and received her M.A. in English from Southern Methodist University. She has worked as a television reporter for network affiliates in Northern California, Seattle, and Dallas. Her work has been published in *Women Writers/Women's Books*, *Story Magazine*, *Other People's Flowers*, *The Wrath-Bearing Tree*, *The Manifest-Station*, *Brevity*, the *Boston Globe*, *1859 Oregon's Magazine*, *Flash Fiction Magazine*, *Bend Lifestyle Magazine*, and BLUNTmoms.

LIDIA KOSK is the author of ten books of poetry and short stories, including two bilingual volumes, *Niedosyt/Reshapings* (Oficyna Literatow i Dziennikarzy POD WIATR, 2003) and *Słodka woda, słona woda/Sweet Water, Salt Water* (Astra, Lodz, Poland, 2009). Her poems and prose have appeared in literary journals and anthologies in Poland and in the U.S.A. A lawyer, humanitarian, and world traveler, she has visited the U.S.A. several times. She resides in Warsaw, Poland, where she is helping to spread a renaissance of oral-history performance. She presently leads literary workshops and a Poets' Theater.

DANUTA E. KOSK-KOSICKA is a scientist, poet, writer, poetry translator, photographer, and co-editor of the literary journal *Loch Raven Review*. She resides in Maryland and is the translator for two bilingual poetry books by Lidia Kosk: *Niedosyt/Reshapings* (Oficyna Literatow i Dziennikarzy POD WIATR, 2003) and *Słodka woda, słona woda/Sweet Water, Salt Water* (Astra, Lodz, Poland, 2009).

ANDREW LAFLECHE is an award-winning poet and author of *No Diplomacy* (2016), *Shameless* (2016), *Ashes* (Pub House Books, 2017), *A Pardonable Offence* (Pub House Books, 2017), *One Hundred Little Victories* (Pub House Books, 2018), *On Writing* (Pub House Books, 2018), *Merica, Merica on the Wall* (Pub House Books, 2019), and *After I Turn into Alcohol* (Cyberwit, 2019). His work uses a conversational style of language to blend social criticism, philosophical reflection, explicit prose, and black comedy. Lafleche is the editor of *Gravitas Poetry*. He was awarded an M.A. in Creative and Critical Writing from the University of Gloucestershire in 2019. Follow him on Twitter: @AndrewLafleche or visit AndrewLafleche.com for more information.

LINDA LAMENZA is a poet and literacy specialist in Massachusetts. Her work is forthcoming or has appeared in *Main Street Rag*, the *Comstock Review*, *Muddy River Poetry Review*, and the *Tishman Review*. She is a member of Poemworks: The Workshop for Publishing Poets. Linda is fluent in Italian and enjoys spending time at the beach, reading, and writing.

EDWARD LEE'S poetry, short stories, non-fiction, and photography have been published throughout Ireland, England, and America, in magazines including the *Stinging Fly*, *Skylight 47*, *Acumen, and Smiths Knoll*. He is currently working on two photography collections: *Lying Down With The Dead* and *There Is a Beauty In Broken Things*. He also makes musical noise under the names Ayahuasca Collective, Lewis Milne, Orson Carroll, Blinded Architect, Lego Figures Fighting, and Pale Blond Boy. His blog/website can be found at https://edwardmlee.wordpress.com

XIAOLY LI is a poet, photographer, and computer engineer who lives in Massachusetts. Prior to writing poetry, she published stories in a selection of Chinese newspapers. Her photography, which has been shown and sold in galleries throughout Boston, often accompanies her poems. Her poetry is forthcoming or has recently appeared in *American Journal of Poetry*, *PANK*, *Atlanta Review*, *Chautauqua*, *Rhino*, *Rockvale Review*, *Cold Mountain Review*, *J Journal*, and elsewhere. She has been nominated for Best of the Net, Best New Poets, and a Pushcart Prize. Xiaoly received an M.A. in computer science and engineering from Tsinghua University in China and her Ph.D. in electrical engineering from Worcester Polytechnic Institute.

CATHERINE LIEUWEN is an Emmy-nominated television writer, essayist, and former mental health counselor. She divides her time between Los Angeles, CA and Albuquerque, NM.

DIEGO LUIS currently studies history as a Ph.D. candidate at Brown University. His photography has recently appeared in the *Tishman Review*, *About Place Journal*, *Glint Literary Journal*, *december*, and *West Texas Literary Review*.

CHARLES J. MARCH III is a neurodivergent Navy hospital corpsman veteran living in Orange County, CA. His work has most recently appeared in or is forthcoming from the *Chicago Tribune*, *3:AM Magazine*, *BlazeVOX*, *Otoliths*, *Queen Mob's Teahouse*, and others. He was recently awarded third place in Blood Tree Literature's hybrid contest.

MEGAN MCGIBNEY lives in Brooklyn, NY where she is a freelance journalist who focuses on education, the people of NYC, business, and mental health advocacy. She is also an adjunct English professor at two CUNY colleges and Pace University.

JACK BRENDAN MILLER is a poet from San Francisco, based in Knoxville, Tennessee. His chapbook *The Glory Tree* is forthcoming from Bone and Ink Press. His writing has appeared in *Raven Chronicles*, *Snapdragon*, and *Open Minds Quarterly*, among others.

N. MINNICK is the author of the poetry collections *To Taste the Water* (Mid List Press, 2007) and *Folly* (Wind Publications, 2013), as well as the chapbook *Advice for a Young Poet* (David Robert Books, 2020). He is the editor of *Between Water and Song: New Poets for the Twenty-First Century* (White Pine Press, 2010) and *Work Toward Knowing: Beginning with Blake* (Kinchafoonee Creek Press, 2020). For more information, visit www.buzzminnick.com.

KRISTINE ONG MUSLIM is the author of nine books, including the fiction collections *Age of Blight* (Unnamed Press, 2016), *Butterfly Dream* (Snuggly Books, 2016), and *The Drone Outside* (Eibonvale Press, 2017), as well as the poetry collections *Lifeboat* (University of Santo Tomas Publishing House, 2015), *Meditations of a Beast* (Cornerstone Press, 2016), and *Black Arcadia* (University of the Philippines Press, 2017). She is co-editor of *People of Colo(u)r Destroy Science Fiction* and *Sigwa: Climate Fiction Anthology from the Philippines* (Polytechnic University of the Philippines Press, 2016), an illustrated volume which won the British Fantasy Award. Widely anthologized, her short stories have appeared in *Conjunctions*, the *Cincinnati Review*, *Tin House*, and *World Literature Today*. She grew up and continues to live in a rural town in southern Philippines.

AYAZ DARYL NIELSEN is a veteran, hospice nurse, and ex-roughneck (as on oil rigs), who lives in Longmont, CO. Editor of *bear creek haiku* (30+ years/140+ issues) with poetry published worldwide (and deeply appreciated), he also is online at: bear creek haiku—poetry, poems and info: https://bearcreekhaiku.blogspot.com/

SARAH ODISHOO is a poet and writer. Her essay "Germane German: A Lesson in Dispelling" was nominated for the 2015 Pushcart Prize by *Under the Sun*. "Euclid's Bride" was nominated for the Best of the Net Anthology, and "Eat Me: Instructions from the Unseen" was awarded the Best Nonfiction Essay of 2012 by *Zone 3*.

SCOTT PEDERSEN is a writer based in Wisconsin. When not writing fiction, he enjoys performing in a traditional Celtic band. His short stories have appeared in the anthology *Metamorphosis* (Propertius Press, 2019), as well as the *MacGuffin* and *Falling Star Magazine*. His short story "Stuck" was nominated for a Pushcart Prize by *Falling Star Magazine*.

CHRISTINA PETRIDES is an expatriate American living and working on a small volcanic island in the Pacific Ocean, where the palm trees and the magpies are imported, but the rice wine is indigenous and delicious.

PATRICK PFISTER'S most recent books—*Far From Home* (2018) and *North Beach Hotel* (2019)—are available from Spuyten Duyvil Press. He is also the author of the poetry collection *El Camino and Other Travel Poems* (Literary Laundry, 2013). His poems have appeared in various literary magazines. Currently, he is directing the documentary film *Poetry, New York*.

FABRICE POUSSIN teaches French and English at Shorter University. Author of novels and poetry, his work has appeared in *Kestrel, Symposium, Chimes,* and dozens of other magazines. His photography has been published in the *Front Porch Review* and the *San Pedro River Review*, as well as other publications.

RICHARD RISEMBERG was dragged to Los Angeles as a child. He has been working there in a number of vernacular occupations since his teens, while writing poetry, articles, essays, and fiction, editing online 'zines, sneaking around with a camera trying to steal people's souls, and making a general nuisance of himself, which is his forte. He's survived long enough to become either a respected elder or a tedious old fart, depending on your point of view, and he is still at it. It hasn't been easy for any of us.

ANDREW ROSS is a retired writer of scientific and technical materials. In 1970, he worked as a volunteer on conservation projects in Africa. Several Nigerian scientists were working with him. The Biafran Civil War had ended the year before. From the stories of their experiences—on the federal or Biafran side—he conceived the story that appears in this issue. His work has also appeared in *Isthmus*.

MICHAEL SALCMAN, poet, physician, and art historian, was Chairman of Neurosurgery at the University of Maryland and President of the Contemporary Museum in Baltimore. His poems appear in *Alaska Quarterly Review*, *Arts & Letters*, *Hopkins Review*, the *Hudson Review*, *New Letters*, *Notre Dame Review*, *Poet Lore*, and *Ontario Review*. His books include *The Clock Made of Confetti* (Orchises, 2007), nominated for The Poets' Prize; *The Enemy of Good is Better* (Orchises, 2011); *Poetry in Medicine* (Persea Books, 2015), his popular anthology of classic and contemporary poems on doctors, patients, illness & healing; and *A Prague Spring, Before & After* (Evening Street Press, 2016), winner of the 2015 Sinclair Poetry Prize.

RHEMA SAYERS is a retired ER doctor, working on a second career as a writer. She has published more than sixty stories, articles, and poems in the past five years. She contributes regularly to a local magazine and newspaper. She and her husband live in the Arizona desert near Tucson with their three dogs. Their three adopted daughters are grown and off on their own.

MARY SHANLEY is a poet/writer who lives in New York City. She is the author of *Hobo Code Poems* (Vox Pop Press, 2008). Her work has appeared in *Mr. Bellers's Neighborhood, Blue Lake Review, Logos Journal, Hobo Camp Review, StepAway Magazine, Anak Sastra Journal, Shangri-la Magazine,* and others.

PAUL SMITH is a civil engineer who has worked in the construction racket for many years. He has traveled all over the place and met lots of people. Some have enriched his life. Others made him wish he or they were dead. He likes writing poetry and fiction. He also likes Newcastle Brown Ale. If you see him, buy him one. His poetry and fiction have been published in *Convergence, Packingtown Review, Literary Orphans,* and other lit mags.

DON STOLL is a Pushcart-nominated writer. His fiction has appeared recently in *Meniscus* (tinyurl.com/yardtt5f), *Twisted Vine* (tinyurl.com/y76m5jqb), *The Galway Review* (tinyurl.com/y6nxt9nv,tinyurl.com/y4vdsqhe), *Green Hills Literary Lantern* (tinyurl.com y2lfxysm), *Heart of Flesh* (tinyurl.com/th44enr), *Cleaning Up Glitter* (tinyurl.com/w77eg99), and *Literally Stories* (tinyurl.com/y7vf5tsd). In 2008, Don and his wife founded the nonprofit Karimu Foundation (karimufoundation.org) to bring new schools, clean water, and medical clinics to three Tanzanian villages.

BRADLEY R. STRAHAN taught poetry at Georgetown University for 12 years. From 2002-2004, he was Fulbright Professor of Poetry & American Culture in the Balkans. He is the author of six books of poetry and over 600 poems, which have appeared in *America*, *Confrontation*, *Christian Century*, the *Hollins Critic*, *Poet Lore*, and others, as well as in many anthologies. His recent book, *This Art of Losing* (Brickhouse Books, 2011), has been translated into French. His latest poetry book, about his year in Ireland, is *A Parting Glass* (Brickhouse Books, 2014), also translated into French.

MERCURY MARVIN SUNDERLAND is a Hellenist transgender autistic gay man who uses he/him pronouns. He's from Seattle. He currently attends the Evergreen State College, and his dream is to become the most banned author in human history. He can be found as @Romangodmercury on Instagram and Facebook.

SUBSCRIBE

P.O. Box 131, Planetarium Station;
New York, NY 10024

____$12 One-Year Subscribtion (one annual issue)

____$20 Two-Year Subscription (two annual issues)

Please include $4.95 for postage and handling and
enclose a check written to *Lalitamba*.

Begin my subscription with issue number _____

Name_____

Address_____

City, State, Zip_____

Please send a gift subscription to:

Begin the subscription with issue number _____

Name_____

Address_____

City, State, Zip_____

CHINTAMANI BOOKS
www.chintamanibooks.org

Chintamani Books is a 501(c)3 non-profit press that was founded to offer book donations to hospital patients, prison inmates, and the homeless population.

We published our first volume at the request of a dedicated group of detox patients at the Addiction Institute, who had experienced our inpatient poetry-and-meditation workshops and wished to study further. Since then, we have grown to offer good reads in fiction, nonfiction, poetry, and translation. Chintamani Books is also the publisher of Lalitamba magazine.

To submit, please send a proposal letter and sample pages/full manuscript in hard copy to:

Lalitamba/Chintamani Books
P.O. Box 131
Planetarium Station
New York, NY 10024

Please include SASE for reply. If you would like your manuscript returned, please provide postage; otherwise, the manuscript will be recycled.

NOTE: Poetry manuscripts should include at least 65 poems/pages.

www.ingramcontent.com/pod-product-compliance
Lightning Source LLC
Chambersburg PA
CBHW031327170626
46807CB00002B/600